Building Human-Centered Generative AI

Tanmoy Hazra · Kushal Anjaria · Rahul Dixit · Nitesh Funde

Building Human-Centered Generative AI

Springer

Tanmoy Hazra
Department of Artificial Intelligence
Sardar Vallabhbhai National Institute
of Technology
Surat, Gujarat, India

Rahul Dixit
Department of Artificial Intelligence
Sardar Vallabhbhai National Institute
of Technology
Surat, Gujarat, India

Kushal Anjaria
Institute of Rural Management Anand
Anand, Gujarat, India

Nitesh Funde
Department of Artificial Intelligence
Sardar Vallabhbhai National Institute
of Technology
Surat, Gujarat, India

ISBN 978-3-032-21411-9 ISBN 978-3-032-21412-6 (eBook)
https://doi.org/10.1007/978-3-032-21412-6

This Springer imprint is published by the registered company Springer Nature Switzerland AG
The registered company address is: Gewerbestrasse 11, 6330 Cham, Switzerland

Foreword

The evolution of Artificial Intelligence has brought humanity to a defining moment where innovation and responsibility must walk hand in hand. *Building Human-Centered Generative AI* stands as a timely and necessary contribution to this dialogue, offering a profound exploration into how technology can be designed to serve people rather than the other way around. In an age where generative systems are rapidly transforming creativity, industry, and society, this book invites us to pause and reimagine AI through the lens of empathy, ethics, fairness, and inclusivity.

What distinguishes this work is its holistic and interdisciplinary approach. The authors move beyond the technical intricacies of generative models to examine the deeper human values that must anchor AI design and implementation. Through its structured progression—from foundational concepts and ethical frameworks to practical methodologies and future directions—the book presents a comprehensive roadmap for building AI systems that enhance human agency, safeguard trust, and promote equitable growth. It powerfully articulates that true intelligence is not measured merely by computational sophistication, but by how meaningfully technology contributes to human well-being.

The ideas presented in this book also hold great promise for the academic and research community. As AI becomes increasingly integral to education, healthcare, governance, and cultural innovation, it is imperative that future researchers, students, and practitioners cultivate not only technical expertise but also a strong moral compass. This work serves as a bridge between scientific rigor and ethical reflection, inspiring a generation of thinkers to pursue innovation that uplifts humanity and strengthens social good. By embedding human values at the heart of AI development, we can ensure that technology remains an ally in building a just, creative, and sustainable world.

This volume will serve as a valuable guide for educators, researchers, policy-makers, and innovators who seek to align technological progress with moral purpose. It embodies the spirit of responsible innovation—one that recognizes that the future of AI depends not just on what machines can do, but on what humans choose to make of them. I commend the authors for their vision and scholarship, and I am confident that this book will inspire thoughtful discourse and responsible action in shaping the next era of human–AI collaboration.

Prof. Anupam Shukla
Eminent Researcher cum Academician
in Artificial Intelligence (Director,
SVNIT Surat)

Preface

The emergence of Generative Artificial Intelligence marks a transformative chapter in human progress—one that redefines the boundaries between creativity, computation, and cognition. As AI systems increasingly shape how we learn, communicate, and create, it has become essential to ensure that these technologies remain aligned with human values and social well-being. This book, *Building Human-Centered Generative AI*, was conceived with the purpose of exploring this alignment—proposing a framework where innovation in AI is guided not only by technical excellence but also by empathy, ethics, inclusivity, and accountability.

In recent years, the rapid evolution of generative systems has inspired both awe and apprehension. While such technologies have enabled extraordinary advances in automation, design, and communication, they have also raised profound ethical, psychological, and environmental questions. This work seeks to examine these dualities critically. It argues that the future of AI must not be driven by competition for speed or scale, but by a commitment to serve humanity responsibly. A human-centered perspective ensures that AI becomes a partner in creativity, not a replacement for it, a collaborator that enhances human potential rather than diminishing it.

This book is structured as a comprehensive journey through the principles, ethics, methodologies, and applications of Human-Centered Generative AI (HCAI). Beginning with the foundational philosophy of human-centric design, it progressively explores the moral, societal, and practical challenges of integrating empathy, fairness, and transparency into AI systems. The subsequent chapters present methodological frameworks, real-world case studies, and practical guidelines for designing and implementing AI systems that uphold human dignity and trust. Each section aims to bridge the gap between abstract ethical ideals and real-world technological practice.

The interdisciplinary nature of this work reflects the collaborative spirit necessary for responsible AI innovation. The ideas presented draw insights from computer science, psychology, design thinking, and philosophy, demonstrating that the quest for ethical AI cannot be confined to a single discipline. Instead, it requires a concerted effort among technologists, educators, policymakers, and citizens to co-create systems that represent collective human wisdom. This book thus aspires to serve as both a scholarly reference and a practical guide for students, researchers, and practitioners who wish to integrate ethical intelligence into technological design.

We hope that *Building Human-Centered Generative AI* will inspire readers to look beyond algorithms and models, and to consider the deeper purpose of AI in advancing human progress. As we stand at the threshold of a new technological era, our collective responsibility is to ensure that innovation remains guided by compassion and conscience. The human-centered approach outlined in these pages offers not only a vision for better machines, but also a roadmap for a more humane and sustainable digital future.

Surat, India. Tanmoy Hazra
Anand, India. Kushal Anjaria
Surat, India. Rahul Dixit
Surat, India. Nitesh Funde

Acknowledgments Writing a book is an act of passion that thrives on the contributions, encouragement, and support of many individuals. We sincerely thank all those who played a vital role in bringing this work to life and wish to express our deepest appreciation.

To begin with, our heartfelt thanks go to our family for their constant encouragement and understanding throughout this undertaking. Your patience and faith have been our greatest strength.

We also wish to acknowledge the profound guidance and inspiration of Prof. Anupam Shukla, whose wisdom and expertise have deeply influenced the ideas presented in this book. Your mentorship has been a beacon throughout this intellectual pursuit.

Our gratitude extends to the many researchers and professionals who generously shared their insights and experiences, enriching the depth and breadth of this work. Your collaboration exemplifies the true spirit of scholarly and professional unity.

We would also like to thank the Springer team for their commitment and professionalism in turning this manuscript into a published reality. Your consistent support and attention to detail have been truly commendable.

We are thankful to our friends and colleagues for their valuable feedback, motivation, and companionship during the writing journey. Your thoughtful perspectives and constant encouragement have been a continual source of inspiration.

Finally, we extend our warm thanks to the readers of this book. Your curiosity and engagement with the subject matter give meaning and purpose to this entire effort.

This book stands as a testament to the collective dedication of everyone mentioned here and many others who have supported us in countless ways. We are truly grateful for being part of this shared journey.

Competing Interests The authors have no competing interests to declare that are relevant to the content of this manuscript.

Contents

Chapter 1
Introduction to Human-Centric Generative AI

1.1 The Cambrian Explosion of Artificial Imagination

1.1.1 The Dawn of a New Information Era

In the span of a few short months, generative artificial intelligence (AI) erupted from the confines of academic research laboratories and specialized technical communities into the global public consciousness. The transition was not a gradual evolution but a seismic shift, an event comparable in its cultural and technological resonance to the public debuts of the World Wide Web or the first smartphone. For millions, the initial interaction with a large language model (LLM) or an image generator was an experience of profound, almost startling, capability. Here were systems that could draft an email, write a poem, generate a photorealistic image from a textual whim, or debug a complex piece of software code. This was not merely a new application; it was an encounter with a new form of technological agency, a tool that seemed to possess a spark of artificial imagination.

This initial sense of wonder was quickly substantiated by data revealing the unprecedented velocity and scale of AI's integration into the fabric of modern life. It is estimated that 77% of devices currently in use already incorporate some form of AI, and the global AI market is projected to grow by at least 120% year-over-year [1]. This is not a future technology on the horizon; it is a present reality, rapidly becoming as ubiquitous and invisible as the electricity that powers it. The historical parallels are striking. Like the steam engine that powered the Industrial Revolution, generative AI is a "supertool," a foundational technology that amplifies human capabilities and promises to reshape our world [2]. It stands apart from previous technological waves, such as the internet or cloud computing, because it offers more than mere access to information. It can summarize, reason, create, and even make choices, lowering skill barriers and holding the potential to democratize access to expertise on a global scale [2]. We are not simply witnessing the arrival of a new tool; we are standing at the

T. Hazra et al., *Building Human-Centered Generative AI*,
https://doi.org/10.1007/978-3-032-21412-6_1

threshold of a new information era, a period of transformation that will redefine our relationship with technology, knowledge, and each other.

This technological sea-change is not merely a conceptual shift; it is underpinned by staggering economic momentum. Figure 1.1 vividly illustrates this financial trajectory, charting the projected global market size for generative AI. From a market valued at just a few billion dollars in the early 2020s, the sector is forecasted to experience explosive growth. After reaching approximately $20 billion in 2023, the market is projected to swell to over $150 billion by 2027 and is anticipated to surpass an astonishing $400 billion by 2031. This meteoric rise in market value underscores the rapid, large-scale investment and widespread adoption of generative AI technologies across industries, signaling a fundamental integration of these tools into the core of the global economy.

Beyond the sheer size of the market, it is also crucial to understand the dynamics of its expansion. Figure 1.2 details the projected year-over-year growth rate for the GAI market, offering a different perspective on its development. This data reveals a period of hyper-acceleration, with the growth rate climbing from just under 40% in 2021 to a projected peak of over 80% in 2024. This phase represents the technology's rapid breakout from niche applications into the mainstream.

Following this peak, the growth rate is expected to gradually moderate, settling at a still-robust rate of approximately 20% by 2031. This projected deceleration is not a sign of a faltering market but rather a classic indicator of market maturation. As the market's total value expands into the hundreds of billions, even a more moderate growth rate corresponds to massive annual increases in absolute dollar

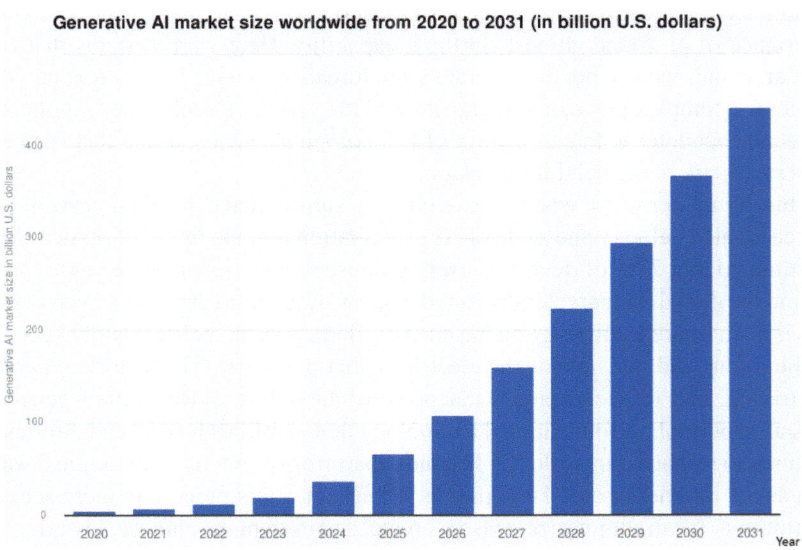

Fig. 1.1 Projected worldwide generative AI market size from 2020 to 2031, in billion U.S. dollars. (*Source* [3])

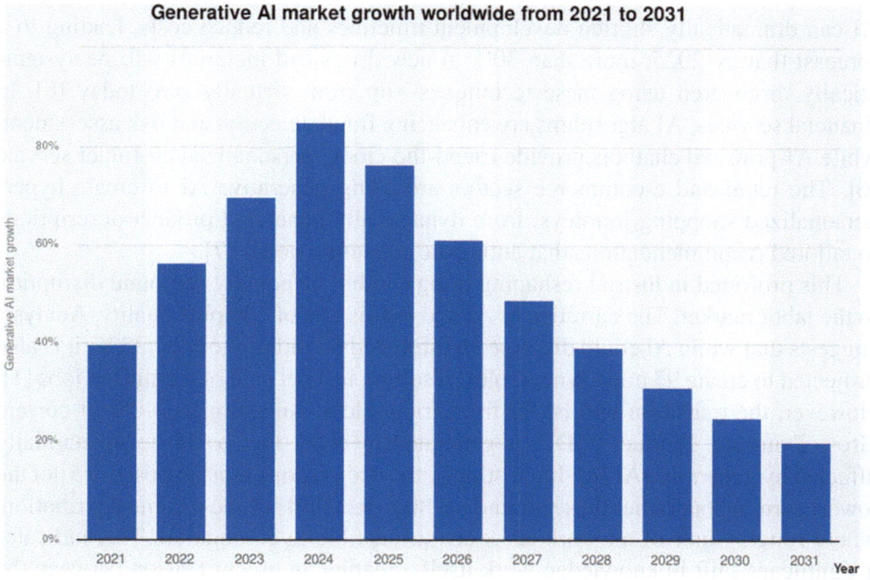

Fig. 1.2 Projected year-over-year growth of the worldwide generative AI market from 2021 to 2031. (*Source* [4])

terms. This shift signifies a technology transitioning from explosive novelty to a large, established, and integral part of the global economy.

1.1.2 Quantifying the Juggernaut: The Economic and Industrial Reshaping

The narrative of wonder is underpinned by an economic reality of staggering proportions. The excitement surrounding generative AI is fueled by forecasts that are driving a global "gold rush" mentality among corporations and nations alike [5]. Projections indicate that AI is on a trajectory to contribute as much as $15.7 trillion to the global economy by 2030 [1]. More specifically, the productivity enhancements unlocked by generative AI features are expected to add up to $4.4 trillion in value annually across the global economy [2]. This is not a distant forecast but an impact already being felt across a wide spectrum of industries. Fields such as software development, marketing, and customer service have seen the highest rates of adoption and investment, leveraging AI to accelerate content generation, personalize customer interactions, and streamline operations [1].

This transformation is not confined to the digital realm. In healthcare, generative AI is poised to revolutionize the painstaking process of drug discovery. By simulating molecular interactions and predicting the efficacy of potential drug candidates,

AI can dramatically shorten development timelines and reduce costs, leading to a forecast that by 2025, more than 30% of new drugs and materials will be systematically discovered using these techniques—up from virtually zero today [6]. In financial services, AI algorithms are enhancing fraud detection and risk assessment, while AI-powered chatbots provide round-the-clock, personalized customer service [6]. The retail and e-commerce sectors are using generative AI to create hyper-personalized shopping journeys, from dynamically generated product descriptions to tailored recommendations that anticipate consumer needs [7].

This profound industrial reshaping brings with it an equally profound disruption to the labor market. The narrative of AI and jobs is one of complex duality. Analysis suggests that while AI could displace an estimated 85 million jobs by 2025, it is also projected to create 97 million new roles, resulting in a net gain of 12 million jobs [1]. However, the transition will be far from frictionless. An estimated 40% of current Gross Domestic Product (GDP) is generated by work that could be substantially affected by generative AI [8]. Interestingly, the occupations most exposed are not the lowest earning, but rather those around the 80th percentile of the income distribution, where roughly half of all work tasks are susceptible to automation. This indicates a significant shift in knowledge work itself, creating an urgent tension between the displacement of established professions and the opportunity to create new forms of value and expertise [8].

The speed of this adoption has created a significant disconnect between strategic planning at the executive level and the on-the-ground reality of AI use by employees. While 83% of companies report that AI is a top business priority, research reveals that employees are already using AI on a regular basis and are three times more likely than their leaders realize to believe that AI will replace a significant portion of their work in the near future [1]. This disparity signals a widespread, "bottom-up" integration of public-facing AI tools that is dramatically outpacing formal, top-down corporate strategy and governance. This phenomenon of unsanctioned and unmonitored use of AI within organizations—a form of "Shadow AI"—creates immense and often invisible risks. Without formal guidance or governed systems, employees may inadvertently expose sensitive intellectual property by inputting confidential data into public models [9], unknowingly use biased tools that lead to discriminatory outcomes in customer interactions or internal analysis [10], or generate content that infringes on existing copyrights [11]. This "readiness gap" between leadership perception and employee practice makes the need for a coherent, human-centric framework not merely a strategic choice for future innovation, but an urgent operational necessity to manage critical risks that are already proliferating undetected within the enterprise.

1.2 A Technology of Contradictions: The Promise and the Peril

1.2.1 The Promise: Augmenting Humanity and Solving Grand Challenges

The immense economic and industrial momentum of generative AI is driven by a profound promise: the potential to augment human intellect, creativity, and productivity on an unprecedented scale. In the workplace, AI is emerging as a "copilot," a collaborative partner that enhances the capabilities of knowledge workers across countless domains [9]. Studies have quantified this boost, demonstrating that the use of generative AI can increase the speed of basic professional writing tasks by 40% and accelerate JavaScript programming by a remarkable 56% [8]. This is the narrative of human–machine collaboration, where AI serves not to replace human ingenuity but to amplify it, lowering skill barriers and democratizing access to specialized knowledge [2]. It empowers individuals to conceive, execute, and refine ideas more rapidly, extending the range and competency of workers and accelerating their time to proficiency [9].

Beyond individual productivity, generative AI is becoming a powerful engine for accelerating scientific discovery and tackling some of humanity's most complex challenges. Its application in fields like drug discovery and materials science represents a paradigm shift in research and development. By analyzing vast datasets and simulating complex systems far beyond human capacity, AI can identify novel drug candidates or design new alloys with desired properties, compressing research cycles that once took years into a matter of months [6]. This capability frames AI as a critical tool for addressing grand challenges in medicine, climate change, and beyond.

Simultaneously, generative AI is reshaping the human experience by enabling a new frontier of hyper-personalization. In education, it promises to move beyond one-size-fits-all curricula by creating adaptive learning systems that tailor content and feedback to individual student needs, fostering competency-driven growth [7]. In healthcare, it can be used to develop personalized treatment plans based on a patient's unique genetic makeup and medical history, moving medicine toward a more precise and effective model [6]. In commerce, it powers the dynamic recommendation engines and personalized shopping journeys that make digital interactions more relevant and engaging [7]. In each of these domains, the promise is the same: to create systems that are more responsive, effective, and finely tuned to the needs of the individual.

1.2.2 The Peril: The Shadows of Progress

For every promise of progress, generative AI casts a corresponding shadow of peril. The very power that makes these systems so compelling also makes them uniquely dangerous, introducing a new class of risks that challenge our social, ethical, and legal foundations. Perhaps the most immediate threat is the systemic erosion of truth. Generative models are capable of producing "hallucinations"—outputs that are plausible, confident, and entirely fabricated [9]. This can manifest as fabricated citations in academic research, damaging the integrity of scholarship, or as dangerously inaccurate product information that misleads consumers [11]. This risk is magnified by the technology's ability to create sophisticated "deepfakes" and other forms of synthetic media, blurring the line between reality and fabrication [9]. The societal implications are profound, threatening to undermine public trust in institutions, media, and even our own senses. Public anxiety is already high, with 74% of people expressing concern about the potential for AI to be used to create deceptive political advertisements [1].

A second, more insidious peril is the automation of bias. AI models learn from the data they are trained on, and when that data reflects our world, it inevitably contains the historical and societal biases embedded within it. Without careful mitigation, these models can amplify and perpetuate harmful stereotypes and discriminatory patterns [9]. In critical applications such as hiring, loan applications, or even judicial sentencing, a biased AI system can systematically disadvantage marginalized groups, reinforcing and even scaling societal inequities under a veneer of objective, algorithmic decision-making [12].

Furthermore, the rise of generative AI has precipitated a crisis of ownership and privacy. The models are trained by ingesting colossal amounts of data, much of it scraped from the public internet, which often includes copyrighted text and images. This practice has created a legal and ethical minefield, as the models can then generate outputs that are derivative of or directly infringing upon copyrighted material, raising fundamental questions about intellectual property that our current laws are ill-equipped to answer [9]. This large-scale data consumption also poses a profound privacy risk. Users should assume that any query or information they enter into a public-facing generative AI service may become part of the public domain, creating significant vulnerabilities for both personal and confidential enterprise information [9].

Finally, these challenges are compounded by the "black box" problem of accountability. The inner workings of the most advanced generative models are so complex that they are often unpredictable, and not even the companies that build them fully understand how they arrive at a specific output [9]. This lack of transparency makes it exceedingly difficult to audit decisions, identify the source of an error or bias, and, crucially, assign responsibility when an AI system causes harm. When an autonomous system produces a flawed financial report or a biased hiring recommendation, the question of who is accountable—the developer, the deploying company, or the end-user—remains dangerously ambiguous [10].

1.2.3 The Hidden Costs: Environmental and Cognitive Tolls

Beyond the immediate ethical and societal risks, the rapid proliferation of generative AI carries significant hidden costs that are often excluded from the calculus of progress. The first is a staggering environmental footprint. The computational power required to train and deploy today's large-scale models demands an immense amount of electricity and water [5]. The global electricity consumption of data centers, driven in part by the demands of AI, reached 460 terawatt-hours in 2022 and is projected to more than double to nearly 1,050 terawatt-hours by 2026. At that level, the world's data centers would consume more electricity than entire industrialized nations like Japan or Russia [5]. The training process for a single large model can consume as much electricity as 120 average U.S. homes for a year and generate over 500 tons of carbon dioxide [5]. This is compounded by the vast quantities of fresh water required to cool these facilities, placing significant strain on local water supplies. The current trajectory, characterized by a competitive race to build ever-larger models, is on an environmentally unsustainable path [5].

A second, more subtle cost is the potential for a cognitive downgrade. While AI is celebrated for its ability to augment human intelligence, there is an emerging concern that over-reliance on these tools may lead to the atrophy of critical human skills [13]. This phenomenon, known as "cognitive offloading," occurs when we delegate mental tasks to technology. Recent research has revealed a significant negative correlation between frequent use of AI tools and critical thinking abilities [14]. Younger users, in particular, exhibited a higher dependence on AI and correspondingly lower critical thinking scores. This presents a deeply troubling paradox: a technology designed to be a partner in thought may, if used uncritically, diminish our own capacity for deep, independent reasoning. The imperative, therefore, is not only to build powerful AI but also to foster educational and professional strategies that promote critical engagement with these technologies, ensuring they supplement rather than supplant human intellect [14].

The convergence of these challenges reveals a systemic issue. The immense economic incentives driving the AI "gold rush" create intense pressure for companies to develop and deploy models at maximum speed to secure a competitive advantage [1]. This imperative for speed and scale directly incentivizes shortcuts that cause the very problems we seek to avoid. To train models quickly, developers scrape the easiest and most abundant source of data—the unfiltered internet—thereby ingesting the biases and copyrighted material it contains [10]. To achieve state-of-the-art performance, they utilize the most powerful available hardware, leading to skyrocketing energy and water consumption [5]. Consequently, the core ethical and environmental problems of generative AI—bias, misinformation, IP infringement, and ecological harm—are not accidental side effects or unfortunate bugs. They are the direct, causal outcomes of the technology-centric, growth-at-all-costs economic model that currently governs its development. This realization leads to an inescapable conclusion: purely technical fixes or reactive, compliance-based regulations will be insufficient. A fundamental paradigm shift is required—one that changes the values and incentives that guide development from its very inception.

1.3 The Fork in the Road: The Human-Centric Imperative

1.3.1 Defining Human-Centric Generative AI (HCAI)

Navigating the profound contradictions of generative AI requires more than incremental adjustments; it demands a fundamental philosophical and practical reorientation. This book proposes that the path forward lies in the adoption of a human-centric approach to AI development and deployment. Human-Centric Generative AI (HCAI) is defined as a framework that prioritizes human needs, values, capabilities, and well-being at every stage of the AI lifecycle, from initial conception and data collection to model training, deployment, and ongoing governance [15]. It represents a crucial paradigm shift away from a purely technology-centric view that measures success by metrics of automation, speed, and efficiency. Instead, HCAI redefines success in human terms: empowerment, equity, trust, and the augmentation of human potential. It is a move from asking "What can this technology do?" to asking "How can this technology best serve human flourishing?" [15].

This philosophy is built upon a foundation of core principles, which will be explored in detail in the subsequent chapter. These principles provide the ethical guardrails and design imperatives necessary to align powerful AI systems with human interests. They include

- **Fairness and Inclusivity**: Proactively designing systems to identify, measure, and mitigate harmful biases, ensuring that AI-driven opportunities and resources are allocated equitably and do not reinforce societal inequities [12].
- **Transparency and Explainability**: Creating AI systems whose operations and decisions are understandable to their users and overseers. Users should have insight into how and why a system produces a particular output, fostering trust and enabling meaningful oversight [9].
- **Accountability and Responsibility**: Establishing clear frameworks that define who is responsible when an AI system makes a mistake or causes harm. This involves building systems that are auditable and traceable, ensuring that there is always a locus of human responsibility [10].
- **Privacy and Security**: Integrating robust data protection and privacy-preserving techniques into the core architecture of AI systems, treating user data not as a resource to be exploited but as a sensitive asset requiring careful stewardship [10].
- **Human Oversight and Agency**: Designing systems that augment, rather than replace, human judgment. This principle ensures that humans retain ultimate control, with the ability to intervene, override, and make the final determination in high-stakes decisions [12].

1.3.2 A Tale of Two Paradigms

The distinction between the prevailing technology-centric model and the proposed human-centric alternative is not merely semantic; it reflects a deep, structural difference in goals, methods, and values. To crystallize this distinction, the following Table 1.1 presents a direct comparison of the two paradigms. This framework serves as an intellectual anchor for the arguments presented throughout this book, providing a clear and memorable guide to the fundamental choice we face in shaping the future of artificial intelligence.

The current trajectory of AI development, driven by the intense pressures of the "gold rush," is on a collision course with public expectations for safety, ethics, and accountability. Public sentiment is clear: 85% of people support a national effort to make AI safe and secure, and an equal number want industries to be transparent about their practices before bringing AI-enhanced products to market [1]. Simultaneously, trust remains a paramount concern for both leaders and employees [2]. A failure to address these concerns will inevitably lead to a "trust backlash," which could manifest as widespread user rejection of technologies perceived as harmful or, conversely, as the imposition of heavy-handed, innovation-stifling regulation.

This is why a human-centric approach is not an ethical constraint on innovation, but rather the only viable path to *sustainable* innovation. By proactively embedding principles of fairness, transparency, and value alignment into the development process, HCAI directly addresses the public's core concerns [15]. It works to build the social license necessary for the long-term adoption, growth, and societal integration of AI technologies. This reframes the entire conversation around AI ethics. Instead of being a reactive compliance burden or a cost center, a human-centric philosophy

Table 1.1 A tale of two paradigms: technology-centric versus human-centric AI

Feature	Technology-centric approach	Human-centric approach
Primary goal	Automation, efficiency, task replacement	Augmentation, empowerment, human flourishing
Measure of success	Speed, accuracy, cost reduction, scale	User well-being, trust, creativity, critical thinking, equity
Role of the human	Operator, user, data point	Collaborator, partner, beneficiary, final arbiter
Design philosophy	"How can the machine do this task?"	"How can this technology best serve human needs and values?"
Approach to ethics	Reactive: compliance, risk mitigation, post-hoc fixes	Proactive: value-alignment, ethical-by-design, continuous oversight
Data handling	Data as a resource to be extracted and exploited	Data as a sensitive asset requiring stewardship and protection
Failure response	"The system made an error." (focus on technical fix)	"How did this system fail the user?" (focus on human impact)

becomes a core driver of competitive advantage and market longevity. It offers a way to break the destructive cycle of the technology-centric gold rush, aligning the pursuit of technological progress with the enduring goal of human betterment.

1.4 Charting the Course: A Guide to This Book

1.4.1 The Journey Ahead

The challenge of building a future where artificial intelligence serves humanity is immense, but it is not insurmountable. The purpose of this book is to provide a comprehensive guide for technologists, policymakers, business leaders, ethicists, and concerned citizens—all who will have a hand in shaping this future. It aims to move beyond high-level pronouncements and offer a clear, actionable framework for designing, building, deploying, and governing generative AI in a manner that is responsible, equitable, and beneficial.

The chapters that follow are structured as a logical progression, building a complete picture of the human-centric paradigm from foundational principles to practical implementation and future-gazing.

- **Chapter 2(Principles of Human-Centric Generative AI Design)**: Having established the "what" and "why" of HCAI in this introduction, we will now turn to the "how." This chapter codifies the core principles of transparency, fairness, user agency, and accountability into a set of actionable guidelines for designers and developers.
- **Chapter 3(Ethical Challenges in Generative AI)**: We will take a deep and rigorous dive into the perils introduced in this chapter. This section will perform a systematic analysis of the complex ethical dilemmas surrounding bias, privacy, accountability, and the potential for AI-driven manipulation and misinformation.
- **Chapter 4(Design and Development Methodologies)**: This chapter bridges the gap between abstract principles and concrete practice. It will explore the technical and collaborative methodologies required to build human-centric systems, covering everything from responsible data collection and model selection to iterative, user-centered design and testing.
- **Chapter 5(Implementing Human-Centric Generative AI in Practice)**: We will move from the development environment to the real world. This chapter will examine case studies and provide practical strategies for organizations seeking to integrate HCAI principles into their products, internal workflows, corporate governance, and organizational culture.
- **Chapter 6(The Future of Human-Centric Generative AI)**: Finally, we will look to the horizon. This concluding chapter will explore emerging trends, anticipate the next wave of technological advancements and ethical challenges, and articulate a hopeful but clear-eyed vision for a future where generative AI acts as a powerful and trustworthy force for global human flourishing.

The future of generative AI is not a predetermined trajectory that will happen *to* us. It is a future that we must actively, thoughtfully, and collaboratively *build*. The choice between a technology-centric path, with its immense promise and equally immense peril, and a human-centric one, which seeks to align progress with purpose, is the defining technological and ethical challenge of our time. This book is intended as a guide for making that choice wisely.

References

1. 131 AI Statistics and Trends for 2025—National University. Retrieved September 11, 2025, from https://www.nu.edu/blog/ai-statistics-trends/
2. AI in the Workplace: A Report for 2025—McKinsey. Retrieved September 18, 2025, from https://www.mckinsey.com/capabilities/mckinsey-digital/our-insights/superagency-in-the-workplace-empowering-people-to-unlock-ais-full-potential-at-work
3. Statista. (2025). Artificial Intelligence—Worldwide. Statista. https://www.statista.com/outlook/tmo/artificial-intelligence/worldwide
4. Statista. (2025). Artificial Intelligence—Worldwide. Statista. https://www.statista.com/outlook/tmo/artificial-intelligence/worldwide?currency=USD
5. Explained: Generative AI's Environmental Impact | MIT News. Retrieved September 1, 2025, from https://news.mit.edu/2025/explained-generative-ai-environmental-impact-0117
6. Generative AI Use Cases Across Industries: A Strategic 2025 Report—HatchWorks. Retrieved September 18, 2025, from https://hatchworks.com/blog/gen-ai/generative-ai-use-cases/
7. Top 25+ AI Use Cases & Applications Across Industries in 2025—The Intellify. Retrieved September 12, 2025, from https://theintellify.com/top-ai-use-cases-across-industries/
8. The Projected Impact of Generative AI on Future Productivity Growth. Retrieved September 18, 2025, from https://budgetmodel.wharton.upenn.edu/issues/2025/9/8/projected-impact-of-generative-ai-on-future-productivity-growth
9. Generative AI: What Is It, Tools, Models, Applications and Use Cases—Gartner. Retrieved September 17, 2025, from https://www.gartner.com/en/topics/generative-ai
10. Legal & Ethical Challenges Facing Generative AI in the Workplace—Forbes Councils. Retrieved September 18, 2025, from https://councils.forbes.com/blog/legal-and-ethical-challenges-facing-generative-ai
11. Generative AI Ethics: Concerns and How to Manage Them?—AIMultiple. Retrieved September 07, 2025, from https://research.aimultiple.com/generative-ai-ethics/
12. Ethics of Artificial Intelligence | UNESCO. Retrieved September 8, 2025, from https://www.unesco.org/en/artificial-intelligence/recommendation-ethics
13. Anjaria, K. (2021). A framework for ethical artificial intelligence-from social theories to cybernetics-based implementation. *International Journal of Social and Humanistic Computing, 4*(1), 1–28. https://doi.org/10.1504/IJSHC.2021.116870
14. AI Tools in Society: Impacts on Cognitive Offloading and the Future of Critical Thinking. Retrieved September 1, 2025, from https://www.mdpi.com/2075-4698/15/1/6
15. What Is Human-Centered AI (HCAI)?—Updated 2025—The Interaction Design Foundation. Retrieved September 14, 2025, from https://www.interaction-design.org/literature/topics/human-centered-ai

Chapter 2
Principles of Human-Centric Generative AI

This chapter highlights the principles of human-centric generative AI design, intending to demonstrate the significance of artificial intelligence in benefitting human needs, values, and experiences. Generative AI (GAI) is growing rapidly and has significantly changed the world of technology, but such technologies' objectives must enhance human interaction and capabilities. This chapter focuses on basic principles and methodologies for new GAI technologies that bring innovations and key properties such as ethics, completeness, and user-friendliness. GAI has received tremendous attention from various communities due to its ability to create new content, explore insights and automated methodologies. Our objective is to make these systems human-centric. This chapter will thoroughly develop readers' deep cognitive concepts on human-centric generative AI and these technologies must offer effective and responsible solutions [1, 2].

Figure 2.1 depicts five basic principles of generative AI. These principles are essential while designing a GAI-driven system. Figure 2.2 demonstrates the essential components of GAI-based systems. GAI is an intersecting area of human, AI, and ethics. The GAI is incomplete in absence of one of the components.

2.1 Framework for Human Needs

2.1.1 Empathy in Design

Empathy is a critical parameter while designing GAI systems. The purpose of designing a GAI system is not only finding solutions to problems; it has to take care of human needs, values, and emotions. The real success of developing GAI systems is enhancing user experiences and trust in GAI systems by including empathy in GAI systems [3].

T. Hazra et al., *Building Human-Centered Generative AI*,
https://doi.org/10.1007/978-3-032-21412-6_2

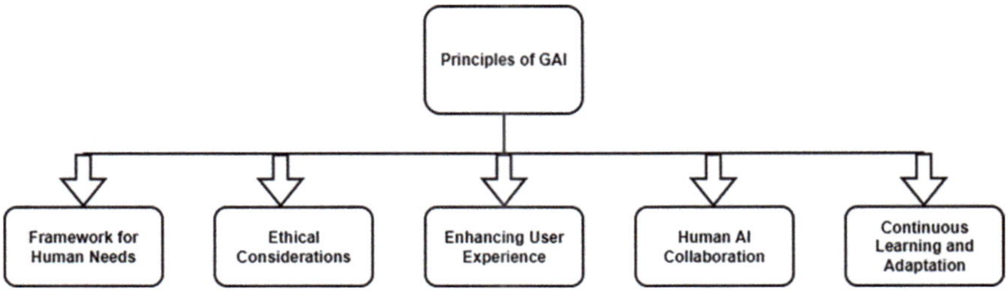

Fig. 2.1 Principles of human-centric generative artificial intelligence

Fig. 2.2 Basic components of human-centered GAI

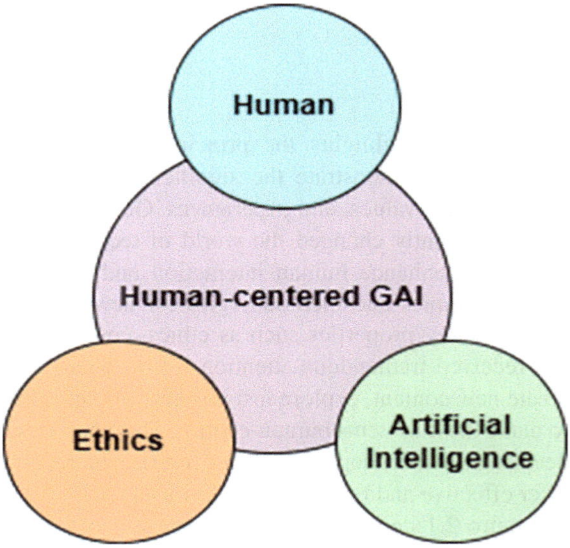

Role of Empathy in Generative AI Design

Embedded empathy in GAI systems reports designers the reactions of users in different scenarios. At the same time, the GAI systems should respond to the users in a supportive and respectful way. For example, a GAI-based chatbot for mental patients should give responses with compassion by judging the state of mental health of the user, and an GAI-based content generation tool should offer solutions to the users by judging their likes and dislikes by exchanging easy-to-understand requests and responses. By embedding empathy in the GAI system, the designers ensure that the developed system will generate bias-free and harmless outputs with high probability. It also supports the users who really need help, and it should also ensure that the system is accessible to those users.

Principles of Empathetic AI Design

Users at the Core: The design of an empathetic GAI system examines the deep understanding of the users in terms of objectives, challenges, and emotions. Such systems can be designed after conducting interviews, surveys, etc.

Context Awareness: Empathetic-based GAI systems need to understand the context of the request in terms of societal and cultural relevance. For example, a GAI system for customer care must process the request made by a customer after understanding the importance and sensitivity of the request.

Inclusivity: Designing a GAI-based system must include all categories of users, including those with special disabilities and unique challenges. The designed system should be fair, accessible, and respectful to all categories of users.

Transparency and Trust: Empathy-based GAI systems should ensure transparency and trust. Users should trust the system, and they should have a clear understanding of the functionalities and capabilities of the system.

Applications of Empathy in Generative AI

Healthcare: GAI-based systems for healthcare should properly evaluate patients' actual requirements and find solutions with empathy. For example, a GAI-based system should support customers with empathy and professional help to build their trust in the system [4].

Education: GAI-based systems should thoroughly understand different paces and ways of learning for learners. A GAI-based system may be able to examine the state of mind of the students by understanding the patterns of queries and provide them with solutions in a lucid way so that they experience a positive, motivated, and trustworthy learning platform.

Support Services: GAI-based systems for customer support should respond to the users in a very humble and polite way irrespective of the behavior and tone of communication and should ensure an appropriate solution to the raised issue. For example, if a complaint is raised due to delayed delivery, the system should provide an apology note, a true explanation, and a quick solution.

Creative Collaboration: GAI-based systems help with art, writing, etc. The system should offer a collaborative environment to the user after examining their inputs. This will certainly improve user's experience and motivate them for future collaborations.

Challenges in Integrating Empathy

It is so far clear that embedding empathy in GAI-based systems will make them human-centric. However, embedding empathy in such systems is very challenging since GAI lacks emotional understanding. Empathy in GAI needs to be verified before it is used professionally. Another major challenge in an excessively empathy-driven system is that it may be vulnerable and may become unreliable and manipulative. GAI's responses need to be ensured to be supportive but not invasive. Moreover, biases during the training may lead to outcomes that may misrepresent various user groups.

Guidelines for Designing Empathetic Generative AI

GAI prototypes should be tested iteratively with real users, and the feedback should be seriously taken for the subsequent iterations. Experts from various backgrounds, such as psychology, technology, sociology, arts, and ethics, should be on the team to ensure the implications of GAI's design in understanding human emotions and social changes. AI models should be trained on a relevant dataset to generate responses that are specific to users. The users should be clearly informed about the capabilities of the GAI-based systems so that they don't have unrealistic expectations from the systems.

2.1.2 User-Centered Research

User-centered research focuses on designing generative, effective AI systems. The idea is to ensure that AI tools understand the needs of users, contexts, and their preferences before offering solutions. The designers need to ensure that the system is properly functional and it takes care of ethical and human values. Finally, the designers successfully establish the connection between advanced GAI capabilities and satisfactory user experience [2].

Essence of UCR in Generative AI Design

Generative AI is used to generate content, ideas, or other forms of output based on the given input. UCR designs the system to ensure that the GAI system aligns with users' needs. It also tries to minimize the risk associated with biased outputs. To resolve these issues, UCR focuses on trust, long-term relations, and satisfaction while designing GAI systems with different backgrounds and user expectations.

Approaches to User-Centered Research

First, UCR will find detailed information about user personas and backgrounds. Personas include the goals, challenges, demographics, and behaviors of the users. Scenarios represent possible interactions between the users and the system. For example, a teacher of a high school prepares notes for lectures using an AI tool, and a professor at a university also prepares research content using the GAI tool [3]. It is very clear from this scenario that each persona uses GAI tools for different purposes. So, the persona and scenarios play a pivotal role. Ethnographic studies define the nature of users in natural circumstances with the aim of understanding natural behaviors. It also includes challenges faced by users while using GAI tools. For example, the system should observe the patterns and behavior of the users while preparing GAI content. Surveys and questionnaires are truly helpful for collecting information from large databases. They help to uncover common patterns, preferences, and problem areas. For example, a survey that collects information from professionals regarding the impact of GAI tools in content generation, plagiarism checking, varieties of themes, etc. Interviews with users provide insights into their preferences, thoughts, challenges, etc. Such types of interviews help designers to understand the needs and emotions of users. For example, a group of artists who are users of generative AI tool for the creation of digital art may report significant issues about originality and creative control. Usability testing is simply purpose-oriented. Users are observed when they interact with the prototype models or newly launched products, the challenges faced by the users are identified, and further scope for improvement is defined. Usability testing is done iteratively so that the GAI system evolves and satisfies user expectations. For example, when testing a GAI tool for music composition, musicians are taken into the pool to identify issues in the tool, and their additional inputs are also considered for this purpose.

Including a feedback system within the GAI framework will help users continuously to give their feedback and share their experiences, which will help the GAI-based framework upgrade its existing version. For example, a generative GAI chatbot can add an important feature to the users: it can provide a rating of the responses that will help the system to refine the quality of the responses.

Guidelines for UCR in Generative AI

To make the system inclusive and accessible to all types of users, users from different cultural backgrounds, demographics, and professions are involved. Experts from different backgrounds are taken into the pool of collaboration to explore the multidimensional user needs. The system design is refined in an iterative way based on continuous feedback from the users. This method helps the GAI-based system to evolve. There should be transparency in collecting user data, and it is ensured that the system follows fairness, accountability, and privacy. The context must be adapted by the GAI-based system for seamless use by the users.

Challenges in Implementing UCR

It is so far clear that UCR is an essential part of a GAI-based system, but it has certain challenges, such as the interpretation of ambiguous or contradicting needs of the users, which require an appropriate quantitative and qualitative method. Another challenge is the gap between the expectations of the users and the required support due to resource and technical constraints. To resolve these issues, the respective organization needs to do iterative research by involving different user groups and to ensure ethical design principles.

Benefits of UCR in Generative AI Design

The discussion on UCR so far has made it clear that it has several benefits. It improves customers' satisfaction by iteratively refining the system design based on user feedback and experiences. It also improves the acceptance rate of the customers and the trust factor. At the same time, it tries to make the system biased and error-free. Most importantly, UCR offers attractive and innovative features that might not have been initially considered.

2.2 Ethical Considerations

2.2.1 Transparency

Transparency is an important basic principle in human-centered generative AI design. The system needs to ensure that users have a clear understanding of the functionalities of a GAI system. The users should have clear knowledge and rationality about the input and output. It will enhance users' trust, help them to make decisions, and encourage users to interact with GAI technologies confidently.

Essence of Transparency

Transparency establishes the connection between human users and GAI systems. By providing clear and accessible systems, designers can explain the functionalities of generative AI and make users fearless in operating such systems. For example, a content-generation tool helps in explaining the generated content with the help of its sources and logic. Transparency also reduces risks associated with errors, bias, and misuse. Transparency is very important in critical domains such as healthcare or legal advice and defense where inaccuracies have no mercy; users may face unexpected consequences. Transparency is also accountable for examining and correcting issues within GAI systems. Users and developers can properly evaluate the ethical implications of GAI outputs when the system's functionalities are clear.

Principles of Transparent AI Design

Explainability: AI's decision-making process must be understandable to users. For example, a generative AI model for content generation must explain the grammar rules or styles used in the content.

Disclosure for Data Usage: Data usage disclosure must outline what data is used by the GAI system, how the data is processed, and, most importantly, how the privacy of the data is ensured. This is ultra-important for building trust. For example, a GAI-based system for recruiting employees should reveal how applicant data is evaluated and ensure that the privacy of the applicant's details is not compromised.

Model Limitations: The users should be aware of the capabilities of GAI-based systems. For example, an AI-generated art tool will not be able to portray culturally inspired content without having any input from the users.

User Control: The users should be given options to control GAI behaviors or outputs. If users can control parameters or share experiences while interacting with GAI tools, they feel involved with the system.

Challenges in Achieving Transparency

Transparency in GAI systems finds methods for simplifying technical complexity with user accessibility. Designers need to ensure that transparency does not provide unnecessary technical details to the users that can lead to disengagement or confusion. Another important point is not to leak proprietary information and intellectual property. The system should reveal only useful information to the users. Transparency should acknowledge and address biases to achieve reasonable outcomes.

Guidelines for Transparent AI Design

It is preferable to use simple language and clear visuals to make GAI functionalities easily understandable and accessible to non-technical users. For example, visuals of decision trees or heatmaps can easily demonstrate how inputs affect outputs without explaining complex algorithms. Users should be authorized to raise queries or notify issues in the GAI-based system through dialogues. For example, adding a feedback button in the AI system helps users to provide feedback that they think is incorrect or inappropriate. Ethical commitment includes how biases in the system are presented and how outputs align with user values. It has already been discussed that transparency can be improved by continuous refinement based on users' feedback.

The updates in user/system manuals and interfaces ensure the GAI-based system is comprehensible and reliable. Transparency-related standards and regulations should be complied with. AI ethics guidelines or data protection laws must not be violated. Clarity in this regard must be present in users and stakeholders.

Benefits of Transparency in Generative AI

Transparency is an essential point in building user trust. This will attract a large number of users to use GAI systems. Users will be confident in the GAI system for the produced output; they will simply accept it. It will also foster users' perceptions of the capabilities of GAI-based systems. Transparency also builds a bridge between designers and users for better innovations. The users are free to provide their suggestions for better experiences. Transparency also ensures that GAI systems are working responsibly and ethically.

2.2.2 *Fairness and Inclusivity*

Fairness and inclusivity are key points in human-centered generative AI design. Designers should build AI technologies to take care of fairness and inclusivity.

Fairness in Generative AI

Fairness in generative AI means reasonably equal interaction with all users without considering their backgrounds, needs, and demographic features. It ensures that GAI systems do not generate biased outputs or behave differently against particular user groups. For example, a generative AI tool for employee recruitment must evaluate the applicants based on their performance and profile; the tool should not give undue advantages based on demographic characteristics. Fairness essentially requires proper training data, algorithms, and evaluation metrics used in GAI systems. Training data should contain diverse populations for training. Appropriate algorithms must be developed to identify and minimize biases, and evaluation metrics must also consider important parameters such as accuracy, efficiency, and equity [5].

Inclusivity in Generative AI Design

Inclusivity refers to making GAI systems available and beneficial to many users. For instance, a generative AI-based language model should provide an assortment of languages and dialects to serve a multitude of users from various countries or regions. An inclusive GAI system should also take into consideration the needs of physically disabled users. Special care should be taken by designers for interfaces that introduce special functionalities on the screen or provide other input techniques for users with mobility limitations. Inclusiveness must ensure that none of the users is excluded from the advantages of GAI-based systems.

Principles for Fairness and Inclusivity

Adaptability: GAI systems should be designed in such a way that they can serve a variety of contexts and user needs.

Varying Training Data: Varied training data must be utilized to enhance the GAI system's performance. For instance, people of different genders, ages, and ethnic backgrounds must be taken into consideration while training a healthcare tool's generative AI model.

Bias Identification and Mitigation: Proper algorithms need to be designed to identify and correct biases in training data and outputs. Regular audits and fairness testing need to be conducted to ensure fair results.

User-Centered Design: A sufficient number of users need to be involved during the design and testing process of a GAI system. User feedback from various backgrounds will assist the designers in reducing the inclusivity gap.

Transparency: This will give information regarding procedures for dealing with biases and offering explanations for the produced output by the GAI system.

Challenges in Fairness and Inclusivity

It is clear from the discussion so far that fairness and inclusivity are very important properties of generative AI design. It is challenging to maintain these properties in GAI-based systems. Biases in the training data are one of the major challenges. Societal and historical inequalities are frequently observed in datasets, enforcing the outputs with bias. Such biases can only be eliminated by properly handling the datasets and developing algorithms to identify and minimize bias. The designer faces another challenge to ensure inclusivity. For example, managing multiple languages requires high computational resources and linguistic expertise. The problem becomes more challenging to ensure accessibility for disabled users since the existing design needs significant changes in the user interfaces. Determining fairness and inclusivity is complex in nature since different societal and cultural scenarios may have different definitions of fair treatment. Therefore, it is difficult to set universal standards.

Guidelines for Fair and Inclusive AI Design

A diverse group of experts needs to be included to define fairness and inclusivity. A diverse group of users needs to be engaged to test GAI systems continuously to identify and address fairness and inclusivity. Reviews of the performance of GAI-based systems need to be performed on a regular basis to ensure equitable and inclusive properties from time to time. The designers may collaborate with specific communities that are most likely impacted by the new GAI system. Those feedbacks can help designers to make more inclusive technologies. Proper education training programs should be organized for developers and users to discuss the significance of fairness and inclusivity.

Impact of Fairness and Inclusivity

Fairness and inclusivity play a vital role in improving user satisfaction and building trust. At the same time, it also takes care of the goal of social equity. For example, inclusive GAI tools in education can provide individual learning experiences for learners with disabilities, but fair GAI in the recruitment of employees can prioritize workplace diversity. Fair and inclusive GAI systems will certainly ensure user trust and acceptance of the system by users. If users feel that they are considered as an important stakeholder while designing a GAI system, then they will accept the system and will build a positive impact on society.

2.2.3 Accountability

Accountability is a crucial point when designing a human-centered generative AI system. Designers, organizations, and users have to take responsibility for the impact of the GAI-based system. The design and deployment process should take care of the stakeholders' accountability to ensure building trust with end users, maintaining ethical practices, and addressing potential harm caused by the GAI system.

Importance of Accountability

Generative AI systems are applied in multiple domains such as healthcare, finance, and arts. These technologies are very popular and useful. The complex nature of such systems and the chance of misuse of the technology trigger the need for accountability. Stakeholders should be able to identify who is responsible for a particular outcome. The outcome may be affected by the generated errors, ethical breaches, etc. For example, if a generative AI system generates bias for hiring recommendations, then the accountability property of the system will help to identify whether the problem is created by the training data, the design of the algorithm, or its implementation.

Principles of Accountability in Generative AI Design

Transparency: Transparency is co-related with accountability. Developers must provide a clear picture of the training of GAI systems, their functionality, and their constraints. Transparency ensures that developers can evaluate the fairness and reliability of the system.

Explainability: Explainability is also an important property for designing GAI systems. It gives stakeholders a clear picture of how inputs are processed into outputs. For example, a healthcare-related generative GAI model should provide a detailed justification for its recommendations.

User Empowerment: Another purpose of accountability is to give control to the users over AI systems. The empowered users can challenge outputs and correct errors in an AI system.

Ethics Governance: Organizations must ensure that ethical guidelines are followed and the processes are reviewed to ensure that the GAI system aligns with societal values.

Legal and Regulatory Compliance: Accountability frameworks must comply with various laws and regulations, such as data protection laws or industry-specific standards. Nowadays, it is an essential part of any GAI-based system.

Challenges in Accountability

It is clear that accountability is of great importance in GAI design, but it also has several challenges. For example, deep learning-based frameworks are "black boxes." Therefore, it is difficult to explain how the specific outputs are generated. Another challenge is how responsibilities are distributed among stakeholders. Another challenge is that laws and ethical norms are not the same in every region. So, it is difficult to make universal accountability standards.

Strategies for Enhancing Accountability

Explainable AI (XAI) techniques are introduced to make system data flow and outputs interpretable and understandable. For example, a finance-related GAI system should provide clear justifications for its predictions when forecasting financial data. The system should maximize collaboration among policymakers, developers, and users to create a framework that ensures accountability. Thorough testing should be performed to identify critical issues before deploying the system. Audits and stress testing can identify serious issues and act accordingly so that GAI systems perform reliably under different circumstances. Feedback mechanisms should be incorporated into the system for users so that they can report problems in the GAI system. Overall, this mechanism will enhance accountability and improve the system iteratively. Risk assessment is a very important part of any GAI system during its development. Risk assessments include technical risks and non-technical risks, such as societal risks.

Role of Governance in Accountability

The role of governance structures is crucial to ensure accountability in a generative AI framework. Organizations should clearly mention the roles of different stakeholders in the development and deployment of the system. They should comply with legal and ethical standards. Most importantly, governments should prepare regulatory frameworks that ensure accountability measures.

Benefits of Accountability in Generative AI Design

Accountability attracts users to accept the newly developed system. Users receive confidence that developers and organizations are taking responsibility for the system outcomes. So, they can easily engage themselves with GAI technologies. Accountability also upgrades the system in a continuous manner. It also helps to minimize the risks of generating harmful or unethical outcomes.

2.3 Enhancing User Experience

2.3.1 Intuitive Interfaces

The purpose of human-centered design is to include human needs, experiences, and behaviors at the center of the design process. For example, crafting intuitive interfaces is vital for the users to interact easily with GAI tools.

Essence of Intuitive Interfaces in Generative AI

Large language models, tools for image generation, and music generation systems are some marvels of generative AI. Users provide input to these models to generate outputs, which may include text, images, or audio. The system requires an interface to allow users to share their needs with the GAI framework so that it can interpret properly. An intuitive interface helps to minimize the gap between the user's expectations and the GAI's performance. The purpose of intuitive design in generative AI is to provide a simple, easy-to-use, and clear platform to users so that users with minimal technical knowledge can also benefit from it. Intuitive interfaces also increase accessibility and usability so that GAI becomes more inclusive and widespread. These interfaces use common design and interaction styles so that users can easily think and communicate [6].

Principles of Intuitive Interfaces in Generative AI

Clarity and Simplicity: One of the most important principles of human-centered design is simplification of the design for the user. We need to communicate how to operate the system to users through instructions, tips for using tools, or examples. No jargon or too many options should be given; instead, we create a text box with a couple of descriptive prompts, and text-to-image models can work better. The GAI offers visual prompts to improve our result. As a result, it reduces the user's cognitive load, allowing for goal-focused efforts without confusion.

Predictability: Since generative AI outputs can be random, it is crucial to provide feedback loops within the interface that match user expectations. This may be showing examples of the results, previewing our outputs, or delivering confidence scores for what is generated. Predictable and stable results mean that when users interact with the system, the GAI should yield expected and stable results even if the underlying processes are highly complex. For example, if a user scrolls on text, then the model could give suggestions or help in a sort of step progress based on the user's previous inputs.

Personalization: Generative AI should have more intuitive interfaces to identify and adapt to what individual users expect. This may involve adapting to previous conversations, customizing replies, and generating more individual responses. A GAI-based art generator learn the user style preference based on user-entered data or previous artwork could then suggest new design user ideas for the next time. This helps the system become more relatable, leading users to connect with the GAI on a deeper level and thus improving their interactions.

Visual and Sensory Feedback: Implementing effective feedback is crucial to make users believe that their inputs are being seriously taken. In generative AI systems, this can be visual, auditory, or haptic feedback. For instance, as a user converses with a voice-driven AI system, the interface could dynamically represent the AI's understanding. For visual generative models, the interface may show a "progress" bar, suggesting that the system is processing the request. Such feedback provides to users and helps them mental comfort regarding the specific flow of their interaction with the AI.

Natural Language Processing and Conversational Interfaces: The amalgamation of generative AI and NLP offers the best solutions for text-based communication. It is easier to engage users when users can freely converse with AI agents and share their queries or feedback. At the same time, it also improves user satisfaction. These interfaces have to understand queries raised by the user, infer ambiguous queries, and provide outputs in such a way that the user feels like a human. Such communications with complex GAI systems will make users very comfortable.

Designing for Accessibility

Human-centered generative AI design should provide access to people with different abilities and support different types of input, such as voice commands and text-to-speech. Interfaces should also offer multiple languages, easy-to-understand styles, and sensory needs. By offering adaptable and customized interfaces, the designers ensure individual needs so that generative AI is accessible to all users of different types.

Streamlining User Experience with Minimalist Design

For generative AI systems, users might be offered a limited number of choices in every interaction. The objective is not to offer a large number of options to users. The interface should guide users on the steps to follow and offer simple and easily understandable suggestions. This approach will certainly reduce the time and effort users put in. Users should be provided with real-time suggestions and immediate feedback for a better experience. For example, when the user is writing some text, the interface should provide predictive suggestions or auto-filling so that the user's effort in writing a large amount of text can be reduced.

2.3.2 *Personalization*

Personalization in human-centered generative AI-based systems is an important factor in engaging users and enhancing user experiences. It is the ability of GAI systems to adjust their behavior according to the users and interact with individual users based on their behaviors, preferences, and past interactions. It prioritizes the needs, experiences, and expectations of users.

Importance of Personalization in Generative AI

There are multi-dimensional applications of generative AI tools such as content creation, customer recommendations, and customer support. GAI systems should be designed with the aim of generating outputs that are not too irrelevant, generic, or disconnected from user expectations. Personalization should generate a more understandable, efficient, and satisfactory interaction to engage users and build a strong nexus between the GAI system and the user. Personalized generative AI systems can offer more connected, specific, and relevant outputs for different applications such as decision support systems, content creation, and entertainment.

Approaches to Personalization in Generative AI Design

A personalized generative AI system can be designed through continuous learning from the user's responses and behavior. By analyzing past interactions, the GAI system tries to recognize patterns in user preferences and behaviors. For example, text-based generative models try to recognize whether the user prefers formal language or a specific pattern. Accordingly, it generates its responses. GAI-based design tools try to learn the color choices of users and their choices of design styles and recommend designs that meet their expectations. The learning process of an AI-based system can be of two types: explicit and implicit. The explicit process asks users to provide feedback. In the implicit process, the system observes and takes necessary actions/changes based on user behavior. Such capabilities are very impactful and improve its relevance and effectiveness.

The objective of generative AI systems should include personalization features. For example, a GAI tool developed for content creation should understand the type of content the user is expecting, whether it's a casual blog post, academic article, research report, or marketing material; the GAI tool should adjust its structure, tone, and style accordingly. Let us imagine another scenario: a GAI tool is developed for image generation or artwork; the system should be able to provide its suggestions based on the user's location, state of mind, current project, or current trends. Context-aware personalization involves various factors such as user goals, environmental influence, and purpose of task that determine the behavior of GAI. This dynamic and user-centered GAI-based system will get more user attention.

Generative AI can offer personalization features by creating user profiles. These profiles usually contain different details of the users, such as their preferences, experiences from past interactions, and behaviors. Generative AI tools will consider details of user profiles when they generate content or provide recommendations. For example, a generative AI tool that generates music tries to learn users' preferences, such as genre, instrument, and tempo, to meet their expectations. User profiles can be constructed using two possible ways: explicit and implicit. Explicit profile building is like asking the user to finish a simple and easy-to-understand survey about their preferences or goals before their interaction with the tool. On the other hand, implicit profile building means understanding behavior and collecting information based on current interactions. By creating personalized profiles, GAI systems offer experiences to users that feel both relevant and dynamic.

Another alternative approach for personalization for generative AI systems is incorporating a feedback loop where users can guide, correct, and recommend changes to GAI's outputs. This feedback will certainly help the GAI system to understand the user's expectations or preferences in-depth and modify outputs accordingly. For example, users can provide their feedback on the quality of generated text by GAI tool and may ask for certain corrections or changes. The GAI tool will update itself using this iterative process and will build trust between the user and GAI. It allows users to experience that they have control over the GAI's actions and outputs. Therefore, a GAI system will behave with users more collaboratively and less like a "black box."

Benefits of Personalization in Generative AI

When users experience a GAI-based system giving them privileges and meeting their needs. Then, they feel comfortable and are more likely to interact with the system. This will build a strong nexus between GAI and the user. This satisfying engagement will build trust, and users feel the system is working for them only instead of generating generalized solutions for all users. A personalized generative AI system is capable to reduce users' time significantly by minimizing the amount of input needed to generate desired outputs of users. For example, a personalized content generation AI-based tool that understands the user's behaviors, goals, tones, and state of mind can generate content more quickly and effectively than a generic AI model. More the GAI system learns from the user, more it predicts accurately. Thus, it minimizes the need for manual modifications or corrections. Generative AI-based systems in creative domains provide personalization in a manner that they enable the user's individual artistic vision. For instance, a visual design program attempts to get to know a user's tastes so that it can aptly suggest designs to the user. It follows his/her personal style, new concepts, etc. Alternatively, custom GAI-based writing applications can assist users to produce content according to their message and voice. It enables them to write more creatively and efficiently. Personalization is a key characteristic of generative AI. But it needs to address ethical issues. The user data needs to be handled ethically, and the user needs to be given consent prior to using them. The user needs to know about data usage, which is referred to as transparency. GAI systems need to provide privacy and security. User information is utilized for enhancing user experience, but it should not be breached.

2.4 Human-AI Collaboration

2.4.1 Augmentation, Not Replacement

Augmentation is one of the key principles of human-centered generative AI design. The purpose of generative AI should be to support and augment human abilities, not replace them from the equation. GAI should not fully substitute human decision-making, creativity, or knowledge; it should be designed to enhance human potential. This concept will definitely complement human-centered design to make users stronger and work with them. The enhancement guarantees that GAI systems ought to be given partner status.

They will augment human creativity, decision-making capabilities, and productivity but not substitute the worth that is brought by humans. This will create sustainable GAI in which users are empowered and user-focused during the interaction with the system. For instance, a generative AI content creation tool can help users by suggesting fundamental ideas or writing parts of a text. But the author needs to be held accountable for completing the text so that it is up to his/her standards. Another such example is generative AI software for a design that may be able to provide different colors or layouts, but the designer (user) will have to make the ultimate choices in accordance with his/her domain knowledge and understanding of the job.

Benefits of Augmentation Over Replacement

The collaborative feature assists users to attain control over their creativity availing support from GAI tools to produce numerous variations quickly. The augmentation not only supports speeding up the process but increases creativity as well. The GAI-based system assists users in discovering new things and finding solutions that the users couldn't even think of. It assists users in thinking beyond the box. Through the merger of AI systems with human judgment, creativity is enhanced and made more diverse and more productive.

Another important benefit of a generative GAI-based system lies in its capacity to manage repetitive and low-level tasks at its level so that users can concentrate primarily on more important, complex, or strategic decisions. For instance, consider a data analysis case study where GAI is able to process vast volumes of data with ease, recognize patterns, and infer conclusions, and it saves time enormously while lowering cognitive load. The analysts are free to concentrate on interpretation and decision-making. It is evident that GAI can emerge as an actual aide to humans in dealing with complexity and information overload.

Another benefit of using generative AI tools is strengthening people who do not have expertise in a specific domain. For example, a person who does not have a background in graphic design can still easily use an GAI-based design tool to generate professional-looking graphics by simply providing their ideas. Another example is strengthening a person who does not have any expertise in language writing but still uses GAI-based tools to easily generate well-structured and professional content by providing his/her ideas or creativity. The ability to augment human capabilities encourages and attracts people from different backgrounds and skill levels to participate in various activities that were not open to beginners.

It was already discussed earlier that a generative GAI-based system should not be a black box. Human decisions are essential before finalizing GAI decisions. GAI systems might be sophisticated and effective, but they are ultimately trained by a limited amount of data. Augmentation ensures that control should be in the human's hand. For example, GAI can diagnose the health conditions of patients by analyzing patient data. However, the final decision should be in the hands of a medical practitioner, who can verify the patient's history, current reports, and needs. So, augmentation with GAI insights will certainly help professionals to make better decisions.

Replacement Risks Through Augmentation

In today's world, GAI has penetrated into every field, but it brings fear to people at the same time. People are afraid of being replaced with machines. People are afraid of losing jobs due to the heavy involvement of GAI-based systems in every sector. If GAI enters into every sector and replaces humans completely, then there could be a social and economic disaster. Augmentation ensures that GAI serves as a human collaborator and helps them to enhance their abilities. The ultimate goal is to build a mechanism where GAI and humans can work together to make the overall process better.

Replacing humans with GAI systems will destroy creativity, empathy, and intuition, which are truly needed in many areas. GAI systems still lack emotional intelligence, which is needed in different scenarios.

Human-Centered Design Principles in Augmentation

These are the guiding principles:

User Empowerment: GAI systems must enhance users' control over the tools and output, allowing them to take charge of the process.

Transparency: Users must be able to see the workings of GAI systems, e.g., the data used, decisions made, etc.

Collaboration, Not Replacement: Humans and AI must collaborate for improved performance; GAI supports the user, not replaces him.

Ethical Implications: GAI systems need to be designed to augment human decision-making by adding ethical dimensions and preventing human values from being undermined and biases minimized.

2.4.2 *Co-creation*

Co-creation is also significant when we are talking about human-centric generative AI design. Co-creation engages human and GAI systems to build relevant, personalized, meaningful, and valuable outputs. Co-creation is a consistent and cooperative process managed by both the GAI and humans to create the end product. Humans are not passive; they are active participants who will determine the experience and outputs.

Co-creation in Generative AI

This collaborative process can take many forms:

First, GAI systems may produce immature outputs that are not very relevant and desirable to users, but users can make them more refined through suggestions and adjustments. For instance, a GAI-based content creation platform may produce a draft of an article and the writer may change the structure, concentration, and tone and recommend the AI to produce the content again in additional iterations. The new generated content will definitely be closer to the intent of the user. Users can modify certain parameters or features of the output generated by the GAI tool and control the results according to their desires. AI can provide ideas or solutions, but co-creation will make the outcome more effective since both the user and GAI decide together on the shape of the final product. For example, current music composers are using GAI tools to generate music of different types, but the final composition is made based on the GAI's suggestions and human insight that will consider various factors such as timing, harmonies, and emotional nuance.

Role of Users in Co-creation

The role of the user is multifaceted:

It is a well-known fact that GAI systems are able to generate creative outputs. The quality of the output will be very high if the GAI system is guided by humans. Users can contribute their expertise, knowledge, and contextual understanding to the GAI system so that they can generate the desired output. For example, a GAI tool can be used by a marketing professional to generate advertisements in digital form. The person will guide the GAI system with his/her suggestions on style, tone, and target audience so that it can generate more effective content. Users give valuable input to the GAI system so that it refines its results. Users must be engaged to make creative inputs at each stage. It will prove immensely beneficial for creative industries like art and design, where the user is responsible in decision-making and obtaining good products.

Benefits of Co-creation in Generative AI Design

Co-creation provides a platform that enables both machines and humans. Together, they produce more innovative and productive outcomes than they would be able to produce alone. For instance, GAI is capable of producing abstract images that enable artists to envision profoundly or incorporate them into their own work. It assists them in venturing beyond traditional artistic boundaries. Engaging the user in the creative process builds outputs that meet the user and his/her needs. For instance, in education, GAI-based software can generate study material with the assistance of student's feedback. It will give a meaningful and effective learning experience. GAI is not just a problem-solving tool, but it also works together and empowers the user. Additionally, co-creation engages GAI tools that enable people with minimal skills to do quality work. Co-creation enhances user trust by involving them in the process. GAI outputs are aligned with human goals and expectations to reduce user frustration. The frustration may increase when GAI systems produce outputs that are irrelevant or disconnected from the user's expectations.

Challenges and Considerations in Co-creation

Co-creation faces several challenges:

The interaction between GAI systems and users must be very simple so that the users don't feel overburdened, even if they don't understand the technical concepts of GAI. An easy-to-use interface is to be designed to ensure co-creation does not get affected. Everyone must have access to the process irrespective of their technical skill. Undoubtedly, co-creation is an important feature in GAI-based systems. However, there should be a balance between when to give priority to GAI's decisions and when to trust human creativity. Co-creation allows data sharing, which is a prime concern for privacy and data security. It is very important that GAI systems should be designed without compromising transparency and ethical standards. It must be ensured that user data is used responsibly.

2.5 Continuous Learning and Adaptation

2.5.1 Iterative Design Process

Human-centered generative AI development involves an important feature known as the iterative design process. The function of generative AI is to produce creative content in the form of text, images, and music. The iterative design process makes the GAI-based system utilize user input and develop itself by means of ongoing learning. The design process does not locate the end product at a single step. It is a chain of steps that enables the system to improve based on frequent testing, feedback, and assessment.

Principles of Iterative Design in Human-Centered Generative AI

User-Centric: The end-users are at the center of the iterative design. The process consists of several loops involving sets of user inputs to make subsequent iterations better.

Continuous Feedback: The iterative process operates on continuous user feedback. Feedback is examined to improve further. This might include small changes or redesigning based on user feedback.

Flexibility and Adaptability: In a GAI-based system, iterative design provides greater flexibility to users as well as supports system evolution. GAI systems are constantly being updated and improved according to the feedback from the users. Thus, it provides adaptability too.

Prototyping and Testing: The systematic process of iterative design includes creating system prototypes that are testable and easily refined. In generative AI, the prototypes are tested to identify what does work and what doesn't work, thereby helping the designers to determine key points and areas for improvement.

Iterative Design Cycle in Generative AI

In the first step, an iterative process tries to understand the needs of the users. The generative GAI aims to solve the problem according to the user's inputs. For generative AI, the research phase signifies how the GAI system can engage users and find solutions for them. Once the research insights are achieved, brainstorming ideas and creating prototypes are the key features in the next step. For example, a generative text model can be designed to generate simple content or help users in creating basic content. After creating the prototype, it is tested by the actual users. User testing helps designers to get ideas about the strengths and weaknesses of the GAI. The design team examines the data to check where further improvement is possible after collecting feedback from users. The changes can be in the GAI algorithm, user interface system, user interactive platform, etc. After integrating the changes based on user feedback, a new version of the GAI system is created. This iterative process continues until the system satisfies the users. This is not the end of the process; the system upgrades itself based on new inputs by the users.

Benefits of Iterative Design Process in Generative AI

The iterative design process ensures that generative AI systems are responsive to user needs at every stage. The new GAI system will be more effective and meet real-world needs. Issues with the GAI system can be detected early since the design process keeps performing regular testing and feedback. As a result, larger problems can be avoided. The iterative design process makes GAI systems more user-friendly and intuitive. Several times, generative GAI systems require complex interactions with the users. The iterative design process helps in the continuous refinement of GAI systems. This process leverages innovation and makes the GAI systems relevant for the users.

Challenges in Iterative Design for Generative AI

The iterative design process is a time-consuming process. Each iteration collects and analyzes data, which makes it resource-intensive. Continuous interaction with the systems may cause the user to become fatigued. Sometimes, users may become frustrated if the output is not meeting their expectations after giving their feedback. The iterative design process relies on user input and feedback. Therefore, it can be biased or cannot properly represent the data.

2.5.2 Lifelong Learning

Lifelong learning is very important for GAI-based systems that should continually learn and adapt to new experiences at different points in time. Conventional machine learning models are trained on specific datasets, and they are not changed once deployed. Alternatively, lifelong learning helps GAI systems to learn new knowledge with previous learning, too.

Key Aspects of Lifelong Learning in Human-Centered Generative AI

Lifelong learning focuses on personalization to ensure that GAI systems respond to individual user inputs. Lifelong learning also leverages adaptability by making the system continuously learn from user interactions. In lifelong learning, GAI-based systems acquire new knowledge incrementally without losing old information. This is a key feature in human-centered generative AI, where models must continually adapt to new things in terms of new trends, social dynamics, and user responses without losing previous knowledge. Human-centered generative AI systems learn from data collected from different sources. There is certainly a risk of increasing biases present in the training data. Lifelong learning can play a pivotal role in resolving this issue by enabling GAI to be trained repeatedly and corrected with time. While GAI system learns from real-world applications, they will evolve and meet with societal values, ethics, and regulations. These systems improve themselves through lifelong learning. It is very important that these systems maintain transparency and explainability so that users get a clear understanding of how the GAI adapts and responds to new knowledge. Transparency helps users to give better feedback. Lifelong learning in human-centered generative AI is very impactful when a GAI-based system collaborates with humans. The strengths of human creativity, skill, and intuition can be combined with the high computational power and improvement ability of GAI, which can significantly improve its generative abilities.

Challenges in Lifelong Learning for Human-Centered Generative AI

The first challenge for lifelong learning is the scalability factor. It is obvious that if GAI systems collect more information, then they will perform better, but at the same time, the computational resources required also grow exponentially. To maintain efficiency, developers should develop GAI systems that learn effectively without increasing computational resources or excessive retraining. User feedback is needed for lifelong learning. It is a serious issue concerning the privacy and data security of the users. In human-centered generative AI, it is important to make designs to protect user information. Data needs to be made secure for storage, anonymized, and handled ethically. While achieving human-centered generative AI, it is necessary to balance novelty and stability. As a system learns, the output quality becomes high, and it also becomes consistent and directed toward the user's purpose.

2.6 Case Studies in Healthcare

Here, we provide a comprehensive case study on the application of Human-Centric Generative AI for a healthcare organization in which GAI-based solutions enhance patient care and operational effectiveness. The case study encompasses the methodologies used, several challenges faced, and the results attained.

2.6.1 Introduction

Of late, generative AI has become a highly sought-after technology as a revolutionary tool for numerous industries. One significant industry in which the technology of generative AI is extensively employed is the healthcare sector. This case study introduces the adoption of Generative AI in HealthTech Innovations. Healthcare organizations are able to implement effectively GAI-based models for enhancing patient satisfaction and streamlining administrative tasks [7].

2.6.2 Background

Previous HealthTech Innovations faced several difficulties, such as inefficient administrative procedures, excessive patient wait times, and insufficiency of patient-personalized solutions. The company addresses these problems by applying a Human-Centric Generative AI solution in order to boost patient satisfaction and maximize operational effectiveness.

2.6.3 Methodology

HealthTech Innovations conducts workshops with medical practitioners, administrative staff, and patients to know their real needs and issues encountered. Feedback is necessary in order to look for a GAI solution. The organization works together with GAI experts to create a generative model that is capable of examining patient data and generating tailored health suggestions. The model is trained on numerous datasets to guarantee diversity and precision. User testing sessions are organized to improve the interface based on input from healthcare professionals and patients. The GAI solution is integrated into HealthTech Innovations' current electronic health record system to provide seamless access to patient data for healthcare providers. Training programs are scheduled for staff members to make them comfortable with the new GAI tools and to instill confidence in them that they can quickly operate the technology.

2.6.4 Challenges Encountered

HealthTech Innovations face various challenges.

Patient data privacy must take top priority. The organization must design proper regulations and apply safety controls that must protect sensitive data. For some changes in organization, some of the employees always resist at the start, particularly when implementing AI technology. Consolidating the GAI technology with the current systems presents technical issues.

2.6.5 Outcomes

Overall, the application of human-oriented generative AI in HealthTech Innovations yields positive results:

Improved Patient Engagement: The patients give higher levels of satisfaction since personalized health suggestions are introduced. The patients also have easy communication with the healthcare providers.

Minimizing Waiting Times: GAI technology is seen that automated the administrative process. Therefore, it minimizes 30% patient waiting time for an appointment.

Improved Decision-Making: Medical professionals are greatly benefited through data-driven information provided by the AI system to make improved clinical decisions.

Operational Efficiency: Moreover, it is also found that the company gains a 25% improvement in operational efficiency. It assists staff in working on patient care instead of administrative work [8].

2.6.6 Conclusion

The HealthTech Innovations case study illustrates the significance of Human-Centric Generative AI and how it can revolutionize the healthcare system. Through adequate knowledge of what patients and healthcare practitioners need, the company implements a GAI solution that enhances patient satisfaction and operational effectiveness. The case study can serve as an example to other companies that can leverage the benefits of AI technology, which is effective and human-centric.

2.7 Case Studies in Education

In recent times, GAI has penetrated into several sectors. One of the crucial sectors which is significantly influenced by GAI is the education sector. Particularly, this case study discusses the practical uses of Human-Centric GAI in EduTech Learning sectors. This AI-enabled academic technology is offered by several EduTech companies with an aim to enhance learning experience of students and to utilize instructors efficiently. GAI-driven systems support personalized learning for individuals and streamline teaching workflows.

2.7.1 Background

There were several issues faced by EduTech companies before the deep engagement of Human-Centric GAI. EducationTech faced multiple critical issues such as inconsistent engagement of students in sessions, limited personalized learning support, and dynamic time-based content delivery by instructors. Students with different learning capabilities usually need different instructional contents that will enable them to improve learning outcomes. To deal with such issues, companies adopted Human-Centric GAI technologies to boost student-centered learning and improve user satisfaction.

2.7.2 Methodology

In this section, we discuss the functionalities of EduTech companies in terms of detailed development and integration of the GAI-driven technology:

The company organizes workshops with educators, students, teachers, curriculum designers, and school authorities to receive proper inputs and to explore their actual requirements. The requirements may include learning difficulties of students, conventional assessment mechanism, and instructional challenges. The feedback from all stakeholders is sincerely taken for designing the GAI-based educational technology. Involvement of GAI specialists helps in analyzing student's data related learning. The model evaluates performance of students, learning ability (quick learner or fast learner), and personalized monitoring for study plans and adaptive content. The GAI-based model is trained on multimodal datasets such as subject contents, assessments, teacher feedback, and learning styles to ensure actual performance. Continuous feedback-based system from users helps in iterative refinement of the interface and recommendations. The GAI-based technology is integrated with the existing Learning Management System (LMS) that enables instructors or teachers to automatically generate lesson plans, quizzes of different levels, and learning resources according to the curriculum standards. Frequent training sessions to be accustomed with GAI-based learning technology are organized to help instructors to understand AI-powered workflows. Instructors receive proper guidance from time to time on assessment of AI-generated content, upgrading personalized learning recommendations and real-time and continuous tracking of student progress.

2.7.3 Challenges Encountered

EduTech companies face various challenges during implementation.

One of the major concerns is protecting student's academic and behavioral data in the system. Ensuring privacy in technology is a serious issue in today's world and it takes time to convince people and to build trust of sharing their personal data. Therefore, strict data protection and access control mechanism are essential to safeguard user data. Another major issue is continuous growing job security. Many instructors feel that AI will cut their jobs due to introduction of AI-based technologies. The authority needs to organize awareness programs and hands-on sessions to build trust and to give clarity about collaboration of AI with human to improve productivity. Another technical challenge is integrating AI with LMS platforms sometimes encounter compatibility and performance issues. So, architectural design and technical support are essential part of the system.

2.7.4 Outcomes

Human-Centric GAI brings several positive outcomes. This section discusses some important outcomes.

Improved Student Engagement: Personalized learning system certainly improves student motivation and involvement in the learning process. Students who were earlier struggling to understand concepts in conventional teaching are highly benefitted by GAI driven learning system.

Personalized Learning: AI-generated materials for study and interesting exercises or assignments attract the students. The system also allows teachers to intervene when the students face difficulties to solve problems.

Efficient Utilization of Teachers: Automated assessments, continuous feedback from students, and validated lesson plans significantly reduce teachers' efforts by a significant amount of time and enable them to concentrate on student mentoring and continuous learning.

Improved Academic Performance: GAI-based teaching learning system improves test scores in schools and various academic institutions by making comprehensive decisions and personalized support.

Operational Efficiency: In fact, GAI based system streamlines content generation and improved learning analytics. Therefore, respective organizations significantly improve overall operational efficiency.

2.7.5 Conclusion

The case study of the EduTech companies reflects the essence of Human-Centric Generative AI in the education sector. The company successfully launches AI-driven solutions by understanding the requirements and challenges by teachers and students. It improves learning experiences, supports personalized learning, and improves organizational efficiency. This case study is an important model for educational institutions seeking to adopt effective, responsible and human-centered GAI solutions.

References

1. Floridi, L., & Cowls, J. (2022). A unified framework of five principles for AI in society. In *Machine learning and the city: Applications in architecture and urban design* (pp. 535–545).
2. Shneiderman, B. (2020). Human-centered artificial intelligence: Reliable, safe & trustworthy. *International Journal of Human-Computer Interaction, 36*(6), 495–504.
3. Amershi, S., Weld, D., Vorvoreanu, M., Fourney, A., Nushi, B., Collisson, P., et al. (2019, May). Guidelines for human-AI interaction. In *Proceedings of the 2019 Chi Conference on Human Factors in Computing Systems* (pp. 1–13).
4. Sai, S., Gaur, A., Sai, R., Chamola, V., Guizani, M., & Rodrigues, J. J. (2024). Generative AI for transformative healthcare: A comprehensive study of emerging models, applications, case studies and limitations. *IEEE Access.*
5. Binns, R., Van Kleek, M., Veale, M., Lyngs, U., Zhao, J., & Shadbolt, N. (2018, April). 'It's reducing a human being to a percentage' perceptions of justice in algorithmic decisions. In *Proceedings of the 2018 Chi Conference on Human Factors in Computing Systems* (pp. 1–14).
6. Ouyang, L., Wu, J., Jiang, X., Almeida, D., Wainwright, C., Mishkin, P., et al. (2022). Training language models to follow instructions with human feedback. *Advances in Neural Information Processing Systems, 35*, 27730–27744.
7. Rahman, M. A., Victoros, E., Ernest, J., Davis, R., Shanjana, Y., & Islam, M. R. (2024). Impact of artificial intelligence (AI) technology in healthcare sector: a critical evaluation of both sides of the coin. *Clinical Pathology*, *17*, 2632010X241226887.
8. Kumar, P. (2024). Transforming patient access through Gen AI and analytics: A path to improved healthcare delivery (published in linkedin).

Chapter 3
Ethical Challenges in Generative AI

This chapter, Ethical Challenges in Generative AI, presents many intricate ethical, societal, and regulatory matters that have developed from the massive increase in AI-related graphics, pictures, music, and deepfakes. There is an underlying thrust, however, that focuses on the implications related to equity, or lack thereof, since AI models tend to discriminate against underprivileged stratas in society because of biased or non-homogeneous training datasets. Privacy, consent, and data protection have also received special attention, especially where massive datasets are used to power generative models. The Issues of accountability and responsibility, having been made prominent, tend to pose pertinent queries concerning who is to blame where harmful outputs have been generated by AI. Moreover, there seems to be ongoing discussions concerning whether it is possible to misuse new-age generative models designed to manipulate users, maliciously disseminate information, and dissolve volatile digital content trust.

3.1 Introduction

There is a dramatic change observed in the field of artificial intelligence with the growing trend of Generative AI, which assists the computer to produce images, text, music, code, and other forms of content themselves. Such innovations have led to a series of opportunities for diverse fields, but at the same time, some challenges have also been identified, for example, originality [1]. With the background understanding of human-centric paradigms, the development of GAI not only measures the result based on performance or efficiency but rather focuses upon the human aspects, norms, and ethical guidelines to be followed. One significant aspect of ethics is that the innovation should be identified and critiqued using this element, especially for those components which generate content. In the background understanding of Generative AI, ethics are not only identified and critiqued based upon the outcomes

T. Hazra et al., *Building Human-Centered Generative AI*,
https://doi.org/10.1007/978-3-032-21412-6_3

but rather upon the components, for example, the intention of the algorithm, the dataset, the intent, which could result in the genesis of the outcomes, which, if not managed using ethical principles, could further aggravate the inequality or could result in the genesis of new ones [2]. Hence, ethics studies constitute the core of responsible innovation, not some auxiliary concern for researchers and developers. By foregrounding ethical inquiry, the risk anticipation and mitigation of harms could be ensured. This would also include considering how Generative AI evolves to focus on concerns such as inclusion, fairness, and accountability.

This chapter deals with the complex questions of ethics that arise from the increased adoption and deployment of AI systems that generate content-text, images, and deepfakes. It explains the complexity of issues such as bias and fairness in the AI models, which can result in discriminatory outcomes against some groups because of biased data used to train them. It specifies the implications for issues about privacy and security of the data concerned, especially with regard to AI systems that depend on large-scale datasets containing sensitive personal data of individuals. This chapter explains the aspects of responsibility and accountability, and addresses issues of liability for misuse and problematic outputs by AI systems. The chapter also deals with the manipulation of AI systems by users and misguiding them, with the integrity of the information and its consequences with respect to digital content. Lastly, it indicates the need for an ethical framework with aims of reducing risks in the development and deployment of GAI systems that are aligned with human rights, dignity, and social values by exploring new case studies involved in failures by AI systems. Thus, this chapter outlines an ethical framework based on these issues that could be addressed in its development and deployment. Also, methodological approaches are outlined on how researchers could be involved in addressing issues of ethics in research in an interdisciplinary context. The empirical procedures, processes, and other insights into designing an AI system need to be adapted from an ethics perspective. The pedagogies dealing with integrating an AI system into an academic curriculum need to be identified which open research area of study.

3.2 Foundations of Generative AI and Its Alignment with Human Ethics

Generative AI is a form of artificial intelligence, which is experiencing a tremendous power of producing new contents according to patterns learned from a dataset. Generative AI encompasses algorithms including Generative Adversarial Networks (GANs), Diffusion Models, AutoEncoders, or large-scale language models (LLM) including GPT, transformers, etc., in the category of Generative AI technologies [3]. These models are deployed in diverse disciplines in terms of applications such as creative art, writing and music, reconstruction of digital heritage and code synthesis. The utility of GAI is growing rapidly; however, the foundation of models developed is based on statistical learning from large, uncurated datasets which raises questions about originality, authenticity, and ethics issues. The researchers need an understanding of the learning mechanism and architecture of these models, along with an evaluation of their socio-ethical impact. The creators should be aware of ethical impact on society.

The ethical discourse debate around artificial intelligence is rooted in philosophy, from duty and obligation, virtue ethics, and utilitarianism. Such thoughts are regarded as framework through which decisions pertaining to right or wrong in the context of AI are made. Moreover, the concepts of fairness, transparency, and accountability must not be made secondary in the discussion surrounding GAI. Justification for analyzing a given technology in light of not merely what the technology does but also in light of the kind of world it creates. The researchers can consider these situations within traditions in their studies which are broader in moral and intellectual context including technical evaluations.

HCAI, also termed as human-centered AI, refers to an AI design process that takes into account "human dignity, autonomy, and values at every stage of the AI life cycle." Indeed, HCAI is an "extension of human–computer interaction research." In generative AI, systems should be able to produce high-quality outputs while taking into consideration the user's intent, cultural traits, social class, and equality among people. Balance should be struck between providing outputs and assisting users to understand change, question, or modify system outputs. A human-centered approach sees people not as consumers of generative outputs, but as co-creators, critics, and stewards of the outputs of meaning. An ethical AI will accomplish social good, and this principle helps forgoing the socially harmful, reductionist performance-focused AI thinking.

Even with the best efforts, aligning Generative AI with human considerations is very difficult. One of the leading reasons is the data utilized to train generative models is rife with bias, stereotypes, and cultural inequity, all of which the models are programmed to replicate. Not to mention, human values are not designated to a singular context, but rather situated, evolving, and often subject to disagreement, making them troublesome to encode into static algorithms. With the ever-growing AI development and industry, there is also a dire need to shift ethical concerns and societal expectations into the foreground instead of prioritizing the algorithms, indicators of output, and monetization. What is more, there is a complete absence of cooperation across disciplines, such as ethicists and technologists, which would facilitate sophisticated, anthropocentric design. In the domain of theoretical scholarship, particularly within master's and doctoral programs, the need to understand these tensions as well as adopt participatory and reflective strategies to ethnographic approaches for generative system design is critical.

Although the Generative AI is clearly revolutionary, it is important to consider the issue from an ethical and human-centered approach. Understanding how the systems work is the simplest part of the issue, while ensuring that the systems work for and with humans is the greater task. Through the human-centered approach, developers and researchers are able to design effective systems that demonstrate greater sensitivity to the social environment and humans. Through this, I hope to have prepared doctoral and graduate students to effectually consider and analyze the issues that are involved from an ethical point of view. As the development of the generative models is continuing, the approaches to evaluating the models and the effect they may or can have on humanity should and must be of greater attention and sophistication.

The methods for the ethical, human-centric development of Generative AI require the integration of diverse disciplines of study, which are not restricted to computer science, sociology, philosophy, law, design, or the arts [3]. As scholars studying this field of study, the aspect of reflexivity, or taking a reflective look at the assumption of impact, arises as significantly important. The graduate studies must be more flexible, integrating different disciplines, but must also cover ethical foundations as well as skills. It is necessary to concentrate upon the cultural perspective of the stakeholders, their significant social aspects, as well as what social frameworks work best for the social group that the AI serves. The development of synergy, incorporating the social aspect, improves the believability or accountability of AI as a tool for the generation of aspects. The doctoral study further benefits as different cases are developed, as well as interventions related to design, along with innovations based upon evidence-based policy interventions.

3.3 Key Ethical Challenges in Generative AI

3.3.1 Data Privacy, Consent, and Ownership

A massive amount of internet data is normally employed for training generative AI systems, often without seeking specific consent from their original authors. A whole host of pressing questions with regard to specific consent, data protection, individual privacy, as well as informed consent, come immediately to mind when one considers that such training data sets may often include sensitive data, copyrighted works, as well as individual information. Where specific models with the capacity to replicate specific identities, voices, as well as styles are involved, it often becomes rather unclear as to when AI systems can be said to be suitable for use versus when they are to be placed into public domain use [4]. A whole host of traditional notions with regard to data accountability are also often rendered rather moot when considering generative models which are capable of producing specific snippets of entirely fictitious data.

3.3.2 Bias, Fairness, and Discrimination in AI Outputs

The issue is that AI models, being the result of AI frameworks, inherit every bias embedded in their data inputs. These could manifest in many ways, some relating to gender, racial, religious, and cultural stereotypes, unobtrusively immersing in the social structures that are in place today. They could manifest in ways relating to

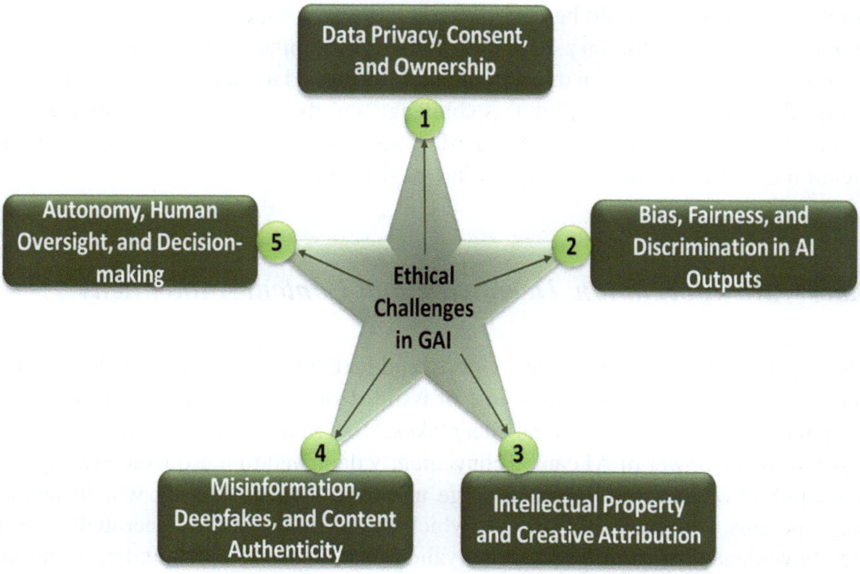

Fig. 3.1 Ethical challenges in generative AI

job-specific gender associations, hateful, and discriminatory language depending on some inputs. However, some methods are being developed by AI researchers for rectification, but most of those methods are retroactive, not proactive, and hardly address anything at a systemic level. The issue here is not merely about technicalities; rather, it is a socio-political issue, where AI model developers and researchers need to be cognizant of data inputs in accordance with how those inputs affect algorithmic outcomes in relation to their respective social contexts [5]. Effective graduate-level AI ethical research would, therefore, be one that includes sociological awareness and fairness audit tools in model development [5]. Investigating fairness is not merely about crossing AI regulations; rather, fairness is about being socially just in AI model development. Figure 3.1 illustrates the ethical challenges of generative AI.

3.3.3 *Intellectual Property and Creative Attribution*

Another area highly contested within Generative AI Ethics is that of inspiration vs. imitation. Where Generative AI models are trained on copyrighted content, it becomes very easy for them to produce work that surpasses similarity levels with previous content, thus raising very important questions regarding who owns what and how we go about crediting people for whatever content has been created. If one considers most people who use Generative AI applications today, it's highly probable that they feel this content is original because of its reliance on previous content. However, it would be very difficult to answer, especially within areas such as art/creative design, literary work, or software development. Unauthorized copying of artwork by authors within this new technology has led to many voices being raised within the community regarding this challenge and its implications within our new world of technology today. Ethics regarding such issues are tracing original content creation and determination of appropriate paying structures.

3.3.4 *Misinformation, Deepfakes, and Content Authenticity*

The capability to generate images, videos, and text at the hyper-realistic level using generative AI has given rise to a host of issues from the perspectives of misinformation and digital deceit. General "deepfakes," forged news articles, and voice dubs assisted by the power of AI can be conveniently deployed to masquerade as anyone, mold public opinion, and even impinge upon the mechanisms by which democracy operates. The pace and scale at which these resources are generated outstrip the conveniences of more mainstream validation techniques, thus undermining the authenticity of any digital data. The current efforts to "watermark" and "track" generative media are in their infancy stages, easy to overpower by those with malicious intent. Moreover, the mere presence of these resources incentivizes the culture of uncertainty, where genuine content is branded as "fake." It is an absolute necessity of the day to find solutions to mitigate the trust deficit in the context of the current generation's age of misinformation.

3.3.5 *Autonomy, Human Oversight, and Decision-Making*

Questions of human autonomy and responsibility come to the forefront with respect to the increasing trend of using generative systems in decision-related systems, such as those in medical or academic institutions and courts of law. Blind acceptance of decisions or suggestions from these systems may imply diminished importance of human judgment and legitimacy of responsibility to flawed systems. Overemphasizing human oversight may imply problems regarding efficiency and cognitive dissonance. This requires skills of exact design and responsibility of systems to develop a balanced mix of human and machine efforts in decision automation systems. To develop a system to maintain human dignity and autonomy and freedom of choice, there is a need to gauge human response and behavior connected to usage of generative systems.

The ethical considerations involved in Generative AI are complex and intertwined, and they are dynamic and continually evolving. Issues of privacy, bias, ownership, disinformation, and autonomy, among others, represent several ethical considerations that can often coexist and complicate one another. To address this, there is a need for a centralized approach to ethical considerations in all institutions. In advanced learning and research, the issue of ethical considerations within generative AI represents a significant emphasis on the importance of being knowledgeable and proactive in addressing these considerations throughout the research process. There is a growing significance of empirical research within Ethics, where consideration is given to what can be achieved both within and through generative AI.

3.4 Socio-technical Implications and Regulatory Policy Perspectives

3.4.1 Impact on Labor, Education, and Knowledge Production

Generative AI technology is revolutionizing the areas of work, education, and creative production by automating tasks that were considered exclusively human domains. In the creative industries, assistive AI technology is being increasingly adopted in design, content production, music generation, and video production, raising questions about employment displacement and the devaluation of human creativity. In the education domain, AI technology can assist in content generation, customization, and student evaluation—but it could also result in a reduced critical thinking capacity among students who increasingly rely on machine-generated content [6]. The very nature of knowledge production itself appears to be transforming, as AI technology has the potential to generate academic content or programming code, prompting debates about authorship, authenticity, and plagiarism. Socio-technical research must explore the dynamic between automation, human creativity, and evolving perceptions about intellectual contribution in AI-mediated environments.

3.4.2 Cultural Sensitivities and Global Justice in AI Systems

The generative AI technology is transforming the realm of work, education, and creativity by automating tasks that were exclusively reserved for humanity. The assistive AI technology is finding its applications gradually in design, content development, music composition, and video editing and raises questions about undervaluing human creativity and job displacement. AI technology may also lead to decreased critical thinking skills of students engaged with content produced by machines [6]. The very process of knowledge production itself seems to be under transformation, given the fact that AI technology is capable of producing academic content or code, thus giving rise to issues of authorship, authenticity, and plagiarism. The socio-technical studies need to examine the complex relationships between automation, human creativity, and shifting attitudes toward intellectual work in AI-enabled spaces.

3.4.3 Generative AI and Psychological Well-Being

The new emotional and psychological troubles are increasing due to the immersive nature of generative content. The generation of personalized narratives, deepfakes, and human like chatbots are blurring the boundary between fiction and reality, which can result in dependency, confusion and emotional manipulation. User can establish effective relationships with AI-generated characters, opening ethical considerations. In the case of children with mental health conditions, these effects can be powerful. The constant barrage of AI-generated, perfection-idealized images, flawless writing, or hyper-productive personas can dampen self-esteem and negatively impact mental well-being. Research in human–computer interaction and psychology must investigate how to design generative systems responsibly, considering users' emotions, context, and psyches.

3.4.4 Algorithmic Influence on Social Norms and Public Discourse

Generative AI systems are constantly undergoing development, thereby significantly impacting the way we think, communicate, and interact socially. Starting from the realm of politics to advertisement and social movements, the use of picture and word-generating tools is amplifying certain ideologies while relegating others to the back burner, all this done without the conduct of any transparent and accountable procedures. The algorithm, which tends to learn from past occurrences, may result in the repetition of certain social ideologies that continue to hold prominence, relegating other ideologies to the background, thereby once again impacting the social norms and the existing patterns of power. Following that, there is the matter of the quantity and quality of the generated material that tends to lead to the creation of an echo chamber, thereby posing significant issues to the world of democracy and media integrity.

These problems also open up a research agenda regarding the critical role of generative AI in both sociological and political scenarios. It impacts collective imagination, helps us understand reality, and also redistributes power in the realm of discourse. Addressing these problems requires a range of interventionist approaches, which extend beyond the technology, including how these tools are managed in the public domain.

3.4.5 *Environmental Sustainability and Infrastructural Ethics*

These generative models, in the background of giving seemingly abstract outputs, work on a massive computational infrastructure, engulfing enormous amounts of energy and natural resources. Generally, large-scale model training-especially based on transformer architectures-contributes to huge carbon emissions and water usage. These are the issues that are always forgotten during discussions on ethics in AI. Further, considering data centers, hardware supply chains, and electronic waste, the environmental impact of AI development has the most significant impact in areas with weak environmental regulations. It is, therefore, a moral responsibility to ensure the sustainability of AI. Graduate programs in AI should include environmental ethics in their courses and actively research low-resource, eco-friendly alternatives for AI. Ethical AI needs to be as conscious of our planet as it is of mankind, and future research will need to confront these pressing issues head-on.

The socio-technical inference of Generative AI indicates that technology is intricately connected with social, cultural, economic, and ecological systems. We cannot depend merely on technical solutions but need examination of design, value systems, and institutional responsibility. This section describes the importance of a multidisciplinary, critical, and context-aware approach to understanding generative technologies that are going to be important for the researchers who pursue doctoral studies. Researchers need to consider how AI systems impact the very fabric of human life, looking into cultural integrity, labor dynamics, environmental sustainability, and psychological well-being. We can strive toward technologies by engaging thoughtfully with the social dimensions of Generative AI, creating content, as well as human dignity, promoting equity, and fostering collective well-being.

3.4.6 *Current Global Regulatory Frameworks on AI and Generative Technologies*

Governments and international agencies are beginning to design legal infrastructure to address the ethical and societal implications of AI technology itself [7]. One of the most comprehensive efforts is, in fact, the European Union's AI Act, which categorizes AI systems according to their risk and outlines legal standards for AI with regard to issues of transparency, accountability, and human control. Other nations, such as the United States of America, Canada, India, and China, are also planning to develop their AI policies, but with varying enthusiasm and scope. Meanwhile, it is essential to note that most of today's legislation remains rather generic and has yet to specifically address the distinctive qualities of generative AI, such as those related to content ownership, the exploitation of deepfakes, or data provenance. In addition, the discrepancies in national policies have also led to "jurisdiction shopping," where companies seek regions with less burdensome policies. As such, researchers studying law and policy must explore not only today's policies, but also the paradoxes that exist between national sovereignty, innovation, and international regulation of generative AI.

3.4.7 Intellectual Property Rights and Legal Policy

Generative AI is beginning to reshape the traditional intellectual property paradigm by poguesing the lines between the realms of inspiration, imitation, and originality. Current approaches on the issue vary from jurisdiction to jurisdiction worldwide, ranging from complete exclusion from intellectual property rights altogether or, on a positive note, an examination of rights models of AI co-authors on works created by said AI systems. Perhaps the most pressing issue here is the training data itself, as popular culture would want us to believe that AI systems that use copyrighted works without permission cannot, in the same breath, be considered derivative or infringing works themselves.

3.4.8 Data Governance, Consent, and Accountability

For generative AI regulation, what is required is a robust data management system, which addresses issues such as data origin, consent, and proper data utilization. The consent mechanisms currently employed, such as general terms of service or no consent at all, just scraping data, do not actually put individuals at the forefront of what is done with their data when it is used for AI machines. Moreover, generative AIs, once produced but later producing biased or offensive content, actually do not point clearly to the producer, user, or the deployer as the accountable party of such bias or negative content creation. Some researchers propose the concept of "algorithmic fiduciaries," which actually carries certain duties and obligations, both legally and morally, akin to our trust belief in health and finance sectors [7]. For further studies, our focus ought to be on auditing and making these systems not just auditable and transparent but also accountable and self-protective against both the customer and the data subjects. The broader objective of these studies is actually ensuring ethical and legal compliance is pursued together, instead of pursuing risk mitigation alone.

As the AI-generated content is increasing in digital spaces, there has been a growing need for content verifiability. Misinformation can rapidly proliferate, leading to serious implications of elections, reputation, and public safety. In order to address this, watermarking, metadata, and blockchain-based attribution tools are being built to assist in content discrimination between original content and AI-generated media. However, to ensure functionality, there needs to be interoperability, tamper-resistance, and industry adoption of such solutions. Not only should ethical frameworks be technology-centric, but there's a definite case to be made for it to address user rights too, regarding knowledge of source, origin, and purpose of user-engaged content. It's essential to raise certain definitional issues for doctoral researchers, regarding trust infrastructure, knowledge, and social-political stakes of unverifiable media. Attributions are no longer a footnote consideration but rather a primary foundation of democratic content integrity.

One of the major challenges of legislating AI involves matching the rapid pace of technological development with the democratic will of all stakeholders. More often than not, discussions in the policy space are dominated by technology experts and corporate interests, leaving little room for the voices of marginalized communities, artists, educators, or indigenous groups. A participatory approach is a necessary condition to ensure the ethical governance of generative AI, one that seeks out different knowledge systems and lived experiences. It could take the form of public consultations, citizen juries, and interdisciplinary expert committees that weigh in on the standards that will determine how AI is deployed. Researchers can make a crucial difference here: They can help translate complex technical information into lucid policy recommendations and even stimulate debate between various stakeholders. Also, policy should be designed to equip scholars not only to understand regulations but also to shape and democratize them: creating a bridge among ethics and ordinance.

While regulatory and legal frameworks are pivotal drivers of generative AI ethics, they cannot do everything on their own. Laws struggle to keep pace with the rapidity of innovation, and sometimes an ethical challenge changes overnight. This identifies and brings forth the need for proactive and forward-thinking governance that weaves law, ethics, and design together right from the start. For researchers, this translates to a policy-aware mindset wherein one does not only contemplate what could be made but, rather, what should be made and under what rules and values. The abilities of legal literacy, interdisciplinary collaboration, and civic engagement are increasingly important competencies in human-centered AI research. Ultimately, this is not regulation as a bar to innovation [8], but as an enabling framework for responsible and equitable technological development.

3.5 Ethical Research Methodologies and Design in GAI

3.5.1 Interdisciplinary Approaches to Ethical AI Research

The multiple disciplines such as computer science, philosophy, sociology, law, psychology, media studies, and design need to be engaged in order to address ethical challenges of generative AI. No discipline alone will be sufficient to understand the complex impacts of AI on society. Rather, by choosing to work from an interdisciplinary perspective, one will be able to analyze generative AI systems not just from the perspective of technical devices, but from those of devices containing multiple value positions, assumptions, and power relationships as well. It implies the need to move from just creating algorithms to reflecting on cultural, epistemological, and

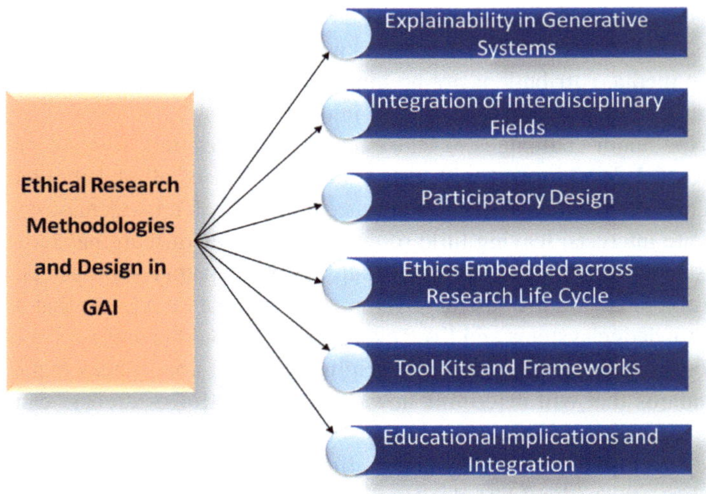

Fig. 3.2 Research methodologies and design in GAI

ethical frameworks underlying the production of the models. Also, it implies the ability to come together to forge a new paradigm of research, highlighting the need to emphasize both technicality and ethicality. Figure 3.2 illustrates the depiction of the research methodology to deal with ethical issues.

3.5.2 Participatory Design and Co-creation in AI Systems

Human-centered approaches have always been the mantra of ethical innovation, and the tools of participative methodologies have proved themselves excellent and fantastic options for engagement and involvement of the end-users, stakeholders, and communities concerned. Within the context of generative AI, methodologies of participative designs assist in making sure that the very purpose, functionality, and interface of the AI system are reflective of and address the needs and values of the people they cater to serve. Working together, whether it is with artists, educationalists, native communities, or disabled individuals, may bring forth some unseen dangers and generate some brand-new AI implementations and applications. The methodologies of these tools of participative designs involve workshops, design sprints, scenario planning, and ethical prototyping. For researchers, these interactions may bring forth some excellent learnings on the very tenets of responsible designs of AI.

Responsible innovation encompasses forecasting ahead of time about the potential negative consequences of using and developing generative AI technologies, often before they actually enter the market. Ethical risk analysis may or may not use several techniques, including AI impact assessments, Value-sensitive Design (VSD), and Ethical Impact Matrices [5]. There are various techniques used for predicting and assessing risk points, which could range from bias, misuse, misinformation, to even psychological aspects of innovation. Impact forecasting encourages innovation and research to go beyond merely evaluating performance and move further into the realms of societal and cultural futures and legality. It requires a mindset that is oriented more to the future and more to complexity and uncertainty, embracing ethical forecasting rather than merely responding to problems. The focus of research needs to integrate ethical impact forecasting into experimentation design.

3.5.3 Explainability in Research

Concerning researching topics in generative AI in academia, we absolutely have to maintain a strong standard of research in terms of transparency and reproducibility. In other words, we should be forthcoming about things such as the model design choices, the source of the training data used, data preprocessing choices, and metrics used for evaluation. Transparency in science isn't a nice that can be satisfied with a publish-and-forget scheme. It is an imperative requirement to ensure integrity and trustworthiness in scientific research. On top of this, we simply can't ignore the importance of explainability, which is the capability to interpret and communicate effectively how these models generate their outcomes for these generative models. This capability is essential in trust-sensitive application domains such as healthcare, the courts, education, and beyond, as pointed out in reference [9]. Researchers can include topics in explainable AI (XAI), auditing of models, and methods to effectively present research findings. Another interesting topic can involve the philosophical limits for the explanatory potential in black box models.

Interpretability is directly linked to the issue of transparency and trust, but generative models like large language models or GANs are notoriously opaque.

Some of the ethical approaches include

- **Model Interpretability Tools**: Using tools like SHAP, LIME, or attention visualization to understand generation mechanisms.
- **Human-in-the-Loop Systems**: Empowering users to query or guide the model's decision-making.
- **Transparency Documentation**: Publishing model cards and data sheets describing model scope, risks, and limitations.

For graduate students, research into explainable generative AI (XGAI) opens opportunities to democratize AI and reduce asymmetries in understanding between developers and users.

3.5.4 *Embedding Ethics in the AI Research Lifecycle*

The entire research lifecycle from problem formulation, data collection, model training, deployment must contain the ethical principles. It includes taking ethics board approvals where applicable, such as institutional review, maintaining data ethics, and articulating the social value and limitations of the research. Tools to support this integration include but are not limited to ethics checklists, AI ethics canvases, and responsible research charters [10]. Finally, researchers should develop habits of reflexivity through the critical interrogation of one's own assumptions, positionality, and motivations. Ethics must be sewn into the very fabric of research practice which emphasize ethical literacy, reflexive practice, and responsible dissemination.

The future of generative AI is not only about the things we create but also how we are going to create them and for whom. In this chapter, we explored a range of research methods and design practices that underpin an approach to innovation that is recognizably ethical and human-centered. We have aimed to foster a research culture that puts responsibility, inclusivity, and foresight at the center through interdisciplinary collaboration, participatory design, and risk forecasting. For the researchers, it is time to rise to this challenge: Not only will you push the envelope on technology, but more importantly, you can start to mold the values and norms that will define AI's place in our world. Remember, responsible research is not a limitation on creativity—it's actually its most profound and meaningful form.

3.5.5 *Toolkits and Frameworks*

A toolkit is a collection of tools, templates, methods, checklists, and that researchers and designers can use to integrate ethics into their AI work.

Examples of Toolkits

Toolkit	Purpose
IBM AI Fairness 360 (AIF360)	Provides metrics and bias mitigation algorithms for datasets and models
Google's People + AI Guidebook	Helps teams build human-centered AI products with guidelines and best practices
AI Now Institute's Algorithmic Impact Assessment Toolkit	Assists in evaluating social and ethical impacts of algorithms before deployment
Microsoft's Responsible AI Toolbox	Offers tools for interpretability, error analysis, and fairness in machine learning
Ethical OS Toolkit	Helps anticipate future risks of technology and develop foresight in design

These toolkits are ideal for researchers who want structured methods to assess fairness, transparency, or harm in their projects.

A framework consists of conceptual structure and set of principles to guide thinking, decision-making, and governance in development of responsible. It is less prescriptive than a toolkit but theory-driven and more generalizable.

Examples of Frameworks

Framework	Purpose
Value-Sensitive Design (VSD)	Integrates human values systematically throughout the design process
Responsible Research and Innovation (RRI) (EU)	Promotes transparency, inclusiveness, and sustainability in scientific work
AI Ethics Framework (OECD, IEEE, UNESCO)	Sets global principles like accountability, safety, and fairness
FATE Framework (Fairness, Accountability, Transparency, Explainability)	Common in responsible AI literature to evaluate socio-technical implications
Ethics-by-Design Lifecycle	Embeds ethical assessments at each stage of model development

3.6 Case Studies

3.6.1 Creative Industries: Art, Music, and Literature

AI tools such as DALL·E, Midjourney, and ChatGPT affect the world of creativity. The tools can generate artwork, songs, poetry, and literature automatically. These tools question how we understand the role of artists in producing artwork and how we value artwork. Some artists view these tools as assistants, while others view them as weakening artistic truth and employment. A major problem arose when digital artists were upset that AI programs replicated their styles without authorization. These types of situations question the role of attribution, authorization, and appropriating cultures. The artists believe that AI programs appropriating artists' work without authorization is about appropriating intellectual property rights. Another problem with generative AI is that it has the potential to imitate the style of living artists as well as those who are deceased, which leads to further authorization and digital identity. The problem of plagiarism, style jacking, and misleading information is vast in relation to the artistic world of literature and music. The devaluation of creativity is also a problem, as it could flood artistic space with artificial entries that reduce the value of authentic artistic creations by artists.

The legal and policy infrastructure has not kept pace with the fast pace of the development of generative AI in the artistic community. The copyright act has struggled to establish a definition of authorship for works that involve agents that are not

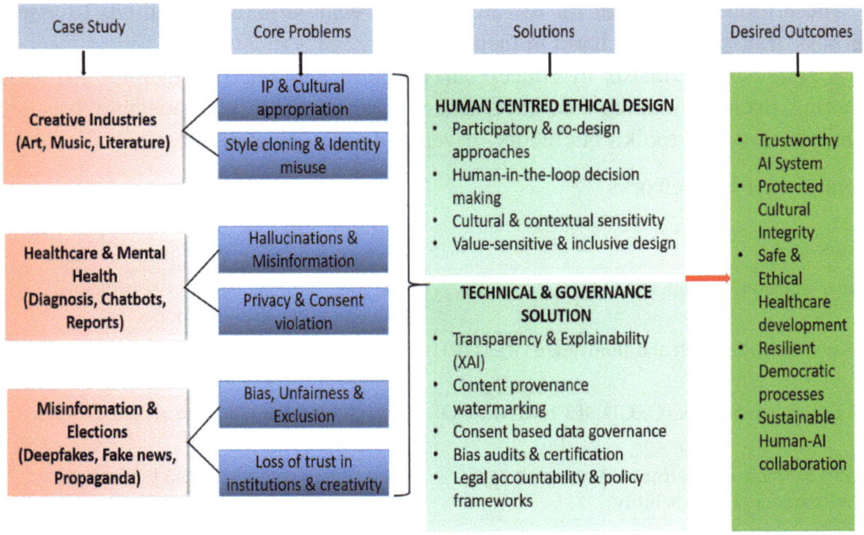

Fig. 3.3 Case study, problems, solutions, and desired outcomes

human and collaborative human-AI productions. There is also a problem of balancing whether AI uses and copies copyrighted material, and the moral rights of authorship, including the right of attribution and against distortion of one's work, in AI-generated copies. Figure 3.3 shows different case studies, their problmes, solutions and desired outcomes.

Nations and creative guilds are increasingly demanding transparency in AI, obligations of disclosure on synthetic content, and a royalty payment structure that rewards original creators.

However, a lack of global equity in cultural regulation and online platform accountability requires that solutions to AI's impact on art and culture prioritize innovation, freedom of expression, and protection within different regulatory landscapes.

Research and design in creative AI must prioritize creative agency and processes of ethnographic understanding in culture.

Participatory design with artists, musicians, and writers must be undertaken to ensure that AI tools enhance and do not drain creative human endeavor.

Design methodologies must comprise ethnographic research, residencies with artists and musicians, and a consideration of AI impact on creative practice and reception of artists' perception of AI impact on their own creative practice. AI and art: fairness in AI training practices requires consideration of equity in representation of cultures and races in visual output and representation of language in linguistic output. Transparency, tracking of content origin, AI algorithms, and style attribution trace innovation and responsibility. Inclusive datasets and open-access creative tools and processes that enhance creative reflection and dialogue processes instead of mere creative automation can comprise a fair AI ethic in art and culture.

3.6.2 Healthcare and Mental Health Applications

Generative AI rapidly changes the landscape in healthcare and mental health through a wide range of applications—from automated medical image synthesis to diagnostics report generation and personalized treatment recommendations, mental health chatbots, and therapeutic content creation. While these innovations promise increased efficiency, scalability, and personalized care, they also surface complex ethical and socio-technical issues that demand critical attention.

Some of the main ethical challenges with deploying generative AI in healthcare regard misinformation and hallucination: clinically wrong or misleading AI advice may cause misdiagnosis or harmful treatments. Furthermore, using patient data to train models (often without explicit consent) raises serious privacy, data ownership, and reidentification risks, especially with sensitive mental health data. There is also bias and fairness: models trained from skewed or nonrepresentative data may reinforce health disparities or marginalize minority populations. In addition, generative model opacity limits explainability, making it difficult for clinicians to trust or validate AI outputs.

The AI adoption in the healthcare sector encompasses not only the technology but also the institutional, cultural, and relational environment within which the technology exists. For example, the role of AI-designed bots offering support in the delivery of mental health services could affect the doctor–client relationship in the sense that affective approximation could replace professional empathy and the doctor–patient relation. Moreover, the use of AI in healthcare could mean the deskilling of professional classes or the automation of the doctor-client relationship, in the sense that computer systems could replace the role of professionals. The availability of generative systems of the type proposed above could mean differences in the availability of the system in urban and rural areas or developing countries, meaning that inequalities in the healthcare system could be widened by the availability and non-availability of the system depending on the location of the country or the availability of advanced healthcare facilities.

Yet, the relevant framework of regulations concerning generative AI within the medical domains still lacks clarity. The various regulations pertaining to medical devices are insufficient to provide a complete framework to deal with the various relevant issues related to AI-generated content. For example, where a mental health bot has adversely affected a client through misguided instructions, whose responsibility will it be the AI bot designers, the organization running the facility, or the client? Moreover, there is also a need to deal with various regulations concerning data sources to train AI. Thus, various organizations are increasingly advocating that AI should satisfy specific safety and ethical audits.

When designing and evaluating generative AI systems effectively and responsibly within the medical industry, researchers and inventors must adhere to ethical research approaches. This involves co-design and research that brings patients, medical professionals, and ethicists together. The researcher also needs to consider contextual parameters that include cultural and medical literacy. Long-term research needs to focus on the long-term behavioral impacts associated with AI treatment, especially with mental health. Ethical considerations within AI need to include value-sensitive design, ethics embedded within AI systems, and continuous assessments. Other methods associated with differential privacy, Federated Learning, and Explainable AI (XAI) need to increase the trustworthiness of the AI systems.

3.6.3 Misinformation, Deepfakes, and Election Interference

The most significant application of generative AI is however its capability in producing the most convincing virtual representations of human beings in the form of characters. These characters were depicted through various forms of input such as text, sounds, and moving images, which subsequently became the chief source of the rampant spread of fake news and propaganda. These contents also include deepfake vidoes that have been used for the impersonation of leaders who have been AI-generated fakenews articles were just some of the means that the manipulators used to create a new public opinion that fit their cause, thus, being the main driver during the elections. One example of such is the footage of politicians' speeches, which, after the elections, turned out to be fake, thus, employees of news agencies became the ones who corrected the mistakes due to the rapid dissemination of fact-checking. These things are examples of generative AI power to destroy trust in democratic institutions and promote unrest among the society. Doctoral students can see this case as an opportunity to access media ethics.

The case studies highlight generative AI's significant influence across various fields and sectors. Each of the case studies describes not only the technological and legal issues but also the human ethical problems which stem from trust, identity, creativity, and harm. A key field of inquiry remains the creation of generative models that are accurate, yet sensitive to social, cultural, and moral contexts. So many current models tend toward generalization across domains, often losing nuance or reinforcing dominant narratives. The next line of systems will need to apply and adapt to user intent, social environments, and ethical standards by incorporating value-sensitive design, user feedback loops, and cultural awareness.

3.7 Open Research Questions and Future Directions

3.7.1 *Emerging Ethical Frontiers in Multimodal Generative AI*

Multimodal Generative AI that combines text, image, audio, and video modalities in a way that achieves very realistic levels of synthetic data now poses novel ethics frontiers that require immediate interdisciplinary investigation. As these models increasingly achieve high levels of complexity and functionality in practice, a series of pressing open questions confront current practices in AI ethics:

- How can we implement explainability in modalities that are opaque even when employing current transparency solutions?
- A related concern seeks solutions that uncover biases emerging in modalities' intersection points using novel methods that are better positioned to grasp their nature and evolution?
- Perhaps most pressing, in what emerging ethics guidelines would we frame consents and protocols that protect privacy during multimodal data set compilations that increasingly comprise unfiltered or unindexed masses?

The future indicates a series of areas requiring integrated investigation in multimodal ethics benchmarks and education in the ethics of synthetic media combined with "cognitive" reasoning profiles inherent in fully "embodied" AI models; a way in which culture sensitivity in data representation must necessarily be ensured if these models are to be effectively integrated across digital platforms in practice.

3.7.2 *Developing Context-Aware and Value-Aligned Generative Models*

A significant area of research is developing generative models that are not only precise but also attuned to social, cultural, and moral contexts. Many current models tend to generalize across different domains, often losing nuance or reinforcing dominant narratives. The next generation of systems must be able to adapt to user intent, social environments, and ethical standards, which means incorporating value-sensitive design, user feedback loops, and cultural awareness. Some key questions to consider are: How can models identify and address value conflicts? How can they learn to recognize local norms without falling into stereotypes? Graduate and doctoral research in this area can pave the way for context-aware alignment methods that promote inclusivity, fairness, and cultural legitimacy in the outputs of generative AI.

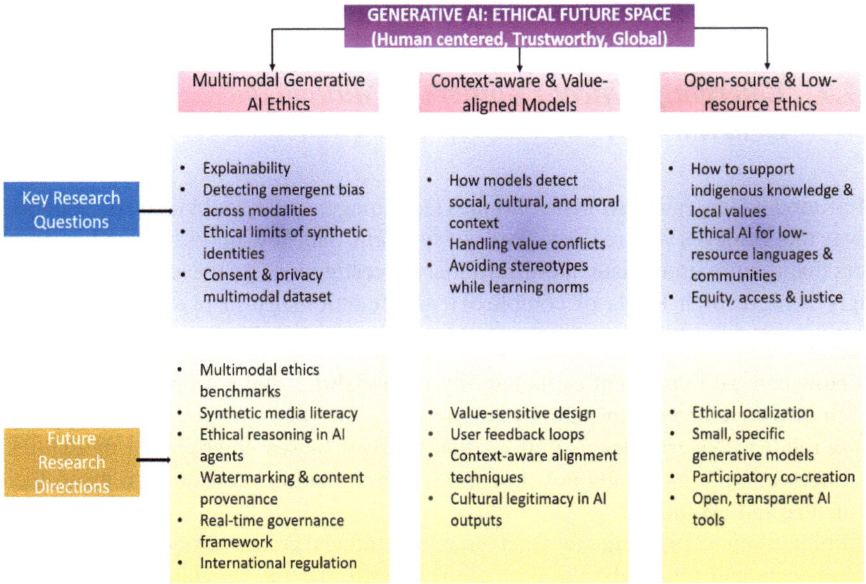

Fig. 3.4 Open research questions and future directions

3.7.3 *Ethical Innovation in Open-Source and Low-Resource Settings*

Breakthroughs in generative AI are more commonly found in well-funded institutions in resource-rich settings, but the use of generative AI with ethical intent in low-resource settings or among marginalized populations is an uncharted territory that needs exploration. Figure 3.4 illustrates open research questions and future directions.

Breakthroughs in generative AI are more commonly found in research institutions in resource-rich settings, but the use of generative AI with ethical intent in low-resource settings or among marginalized populations is an uncharted territory that needs exploration. What's the approach when it comes to employing generative AI for the benefit of indigenous knowledge sources, or doing so in the context of regions that are impacted by a disaster? There is an immediate need for innovation practices that are localized and community-centric with an understanding and respect for the culture. Researchers in this area are critical for shaping the future of equity, accessibility, and justice with respect to innovation in artificial intelligence.

The future of generative AI is like co-creation approaches to global governance and ethical norms, these issues are complex and require immediate attention. It is the duty of the researchers to help create the next generation of human-centric intelligent systems that are not only intelligent but kind and ethical as well. The ethical environment of the field of AI is not defined; rather, it is to be visualized.

3.8 Conclusion

Generative AI is changing the game, in terms of how we create, how we communicate, and how we think about intelligence. This opens exciting new opportunities in art, science, education, and governance, but also entails a number of grave concerns in terms of ethics, society, and philosophy. As apparent from the chapter, the challenges poses go beyond just "getting the tech right; they go deep to our core human values, sense of agency, and quest for equity." Questions of bias, consent, misinformation, creative ownership, and global fairness are magnified through generative AI, often because of existing conflicts it exacerbates or makes more apparent.

For researchers in these areas, engaging with the above issues is not an option but a necessity. Ethics within generative AI is not merely an add-on to the technical aspects of research; rather, it is a very key framework in which responsible inquiry and innovation are constructed. On this basis, by anchoring their research in human-centered design principles, participatory methods, and interdisciplinary conversations, the inclusion of future researchers needs to be oriented so that AI systems should be made inclusive, accountable, and of benefit to society. In other words, the march of progress on the technical front has to be accompanied by the resolve for ethical foresight, cultural awareness, and reflection.

With this chapter, some basic concepts, case studies, methodological tools, and research paths have been laid out for the investigation of the ethical aspects concerning generative AI. Yet many questions remain open, and it's a moving target. The more generative AI is shaping our digital futures, the more important human-centered research becomes. It's through this perspective that we make sure generative AI informs us not just about the world as it is but assists us in building the world as it ought to be: fair, imaginative, and deeply human.

References

1. Suri, C. S., Shukla, S. S., Pal, R., Srivastava, V., Talele, G., & Kumar, M. B. (2024). Generative AI in content creation: Opportunities and ethical challenges. In *2024 IEEE 11th Uttar Pradesh Section International Conference on Electrical, Electronics and Computer Engineering (UPCON), Lucknow, India* (pp. 1–6).
2. Crawford, K. (2021). *The atlas of AI: Power, politics, and the planetary costs of artificial intelligence*. Yale University Press.
3. Al-kfairy, M., Mustafa, D., Kshetri, N., Insiew, M., & Alfandi, O. (2024). Ethical challenges and solutions of generative AI: An interdisciplinary perspective. *Informatics, 11*(3), 58.
4. Raji, I. D., & Buolamwini, J. (2019). Actionable auditing: Investigating the impact of publicly naming biased performance results of commercial AI products. In *AAAI/ACM Conference on AI, Ethics, and Society*.
5. Donvir, A., & Sharma, G. (2025). Ethical challenges and frameworks in AI-driven software development and testing. In *2025 IEEE 15th Annual Computing and Communication Workshop and Conference (CCWC), Las Vgas, NV, USA* (pp. 00569–00576).

6. Đerić, E., Frank, D., & Vuković, D. (2025). Exploring the ethical implications of using generative AI tools in higher education. *Informatics, 12*(2), 36. https://doi.org/10.3390/informatics12020036
7. Pasetti, M., Santos, J. W., & Corrêa, N. K. (2025). Technical, legal, and ethical challenges of generative artificial intelligence: An analysis of the governance of training data and copyrights. *Discover Artificial Intelligence, 5*, 193.
8. Wu, Y., & Wang, X. (2024). Balancing innovation and regulation in the age of generative artificial intelligence. *Journal of Information Policy, 14*, 1–23.
9. Goktas, P. (2024). Ethics, transparency, and explainability in generative AI decision-making systems: A comprehensive bibliometric study. *Journal of Decision Systems*, 1–29. https://doi.org/10.1080/12460125.2024.2410042
10. Ning, Y., Teixayavong, S., Shang, Y., Savulescu, J., Nagaraj, V., Miao, D., Mertens, M., Ting, D. S. W., Ong, J. C. L., Liu, M., Cao, J., Dunn, M., Vaughan, R., Ong, M. E. H., Sung, J.J.-Y., Topol, E. J., & Liu, N. (2024). Generative artificial intelligence and ethical considerations in health care: A scoping review and ethics checklist. *Lancet Digital Health, 6*(11), e848–e856.
11. Suraj, N., Yeran, L., Ruoshui, L., Zoe, Y., & Zichen, H. (2024). Balancing innovation and ethics: Transformative potential and ethical challenges of generative AI in education.

Chapter 4
Design and Development Methodologies of Human-Centric Generative AI

This chapter underscores the pressing need for a human-centered framework in generative AI, emphasizing the transition from mere technical progress to fostering human empowerment, trust, and societal well-being. It explores the foundational transformation introduced by generative models and its ethical implications, while defining the emergence and principles of Human-Centric Generative AI (HCGAI) through a structured taxonomy. The chapter introduces a formal methodology to integrate human values and control into model design via mathematical modeling, and compares participatory, value-sensitive, and human-in-the-loop design approaches. It further proposes pragmatic frameworks for scalable development using Agile and GenAIOps, alongside comprehensive evaluation strategies focused on quality, user experience, and ethical integrity. Advanced mechanisms addressing bias, fairness, and explainability are analyzed across the AI lifecycle. Through detailed case studies in creative industries, healthcare, education, and infrastructure, the chapter demonstrates HCGAI's practical impact and concludes with a strategic research roadmap for future advancements in this evolving field.

4.1 The Foundations of Human-Centric Generative AI (GAI)

4.1.1 Redefining Creation and Collaboration: The Imperative for a Human-Centric Approach

The rapid proliferation of artificial intelligence has reached an inflection point with the advent of generative models. These systems, capable of creating novel content rather than simply analyzing existing data, are reshaping industries and challenging fundamental concepts of creativity, authorship, and collaboration. This technological

T. Hazra et al., *Building Human-Centered Generative AI*,
https://doi.org/10.1007/978-3-032-21412-6_4

paradigm shift necessitates a corresponding evolution in design philosophy. As GAI systems become more autonomous and deeply integrated into societal functions, the development of a principled, human-centric approach is no longer an academic ideal but a critical requirement for responsible and sustainable innovation. This section establishes the conceptual foundations of this approach, defining the generative AI revolution and outlining the core tenets of Human-Centered GAI (HCGAI) as a guiding framework for navigating this new terrain.

Building upon this foundation, HCGAI emphasizes aligning technological capabilities with human values, needs, and well-being, ensuring that innovation serves as a tool for empowerment rather than displacement. It recognizes that generative AI's transformative potential lies not only in its computational prowess but also in its capacity to augment human creativity, support informed decision-making, and foster inclusive participation. By embedding ethical principles, transparency, and accountability into the lifecycle of AI design and deployment, HCGAI seeks to balance technological advancement with societal trust, ultimately steering the generative AI revolution toward outcomes that are equitable, sustainable, and resilient.

4.1.2 The Generative AI Revolution

Generative Artificial Intelligence (GAI) represents a significant departure from traditional discriminative AI models. Whereas discriminative models learn to map input data to a specific output label (e.g., classifying an image as a "cat" or "dog"), generative models learn the underlying joint probability distribution of a dataset and can therefore create new, plausible data samples that resemble the training data. This capacity to generate original content—including text, images, code, music, and video—positions GAI as a powerful technology for advancing both scientific research and industrial applications [1].

The technical underpinnings of this revolution are rooted in several key architectural frameworks that have evolved over the last decade. Early breakthroughs were seen with Variational Autoencoders (VAEs) and Generative Adversarial Networks (GANs), which demonstrated remarkable capabilities in image generation [2]. More recently, the development of Transformer-based architectures [3] and Diffusion Models [3] has led to an explosion in the quality and versatility of generative systems, powering prominent models like the GPT series for language, DALL-E and Stable Diffusion for image generation, and even specialized models like Mamba for State Space Models (SSM) [1]. These models have demonstrated significant commercial value and technical potential, exhibiting emergent abilities in reasoning and generalization across various tasks [1].

The applications of GAI are broad and transformative. They support a range of intelligence-level tasks common to different domains, including content generation, data augmentation, the creation of conversational agents and question-answering tools, and the enhancement of human–machine interactions [1]. In the creative industries, GAI is used to generate art, music, and design concepts, accelerating production timelines and offering novel perspectives [2]. In healthcare, it is used to create synthetic patient health records to improve clinical text mining while preserving privacy [4]. In supply chain management, it aids in forecasting, scenario planning, and decision support [5]. This two-fold ability to perform complex analysis and generate novel content establishes GAI as a foundational technology of the modern intelligence era [1].

Beyond these domain-specific applications, the true significance of GAI lies in its capacity to act as a catalyst for cross-disciplinary innovation, enabling solutions that transcend traditional sectoral boundaries. By integrating generative capabilities with advances in areas such as robotics, IoT, and edge computing, GAI can facilitate adaptive, context-aware systems that respond dynamically to real-world complexities. This convergence not only enhances operational efficiency but also opens new possibilities for personalized experiences, collaborative problem-solving, and sustainable development, reinforcing GAI's role as a transformative force in shaping the next wave of socio-technical progress.

4.1.3 The Emergence of Human-Centered GAI (HCGAI)

The very power of GAI introduces unique challenges. Unlike traditional technologies, GAI systems exhibit unprecedented levels of complexity, autonomy, and personalized adaptive behavior [6]. They can learn, adapt, and make independent decisions in ways that are often not easily interpretable by humans, a phenomenon commonly referred to as the "black box" problem. This opacity makes it difficult for users to comprehend, trust, or challenge GAI-driven outcomes, necessitating a fundamental shift in design and development approaches [6].

In response to these challenges, the field of Human-Centered Generative Artificial Intelligence (HCGAI) has emerged as a guiding philosophy. HCGAI seeks to ensure that GAI systems are designed, developed, and deployed in ways that align with human needs and values, augmenting human capabilities rather than diminishing them [6]. It rejects a purely mechanistic or techno-centric paradigm, instead prioritizing human well-being, control, and dignity. This approach is not entirely new; it builds on long-standing inquiries in fields like Human–Computer Interaction (HCI) concerning the allocation of functions between humans and their tools [6]. However, the unique nature of GAI demands a renewed focus on principles like explainability, transparency, and data privacy [6].

A comprehensive definition synthesized from a systematic literature review posits HCGAI as an approach that "focuses on understanding purposes, human values, and desired GAI properties in the creation of AI systems by applying Human-Centered Design practices. HCGAI seeks to augment human capabilities while maintaining human control over AI systems, by considering the necessity, context, and ethical and legal conditions of the AI system as well as promoting individual and societal well-being" [6]. This definition provides a structured lens through which to analyze and construct these complex systems.

4.1.4 A Framework for HCGAI: Purpose, Values, and Properties

The HCGAI philosophy can be operationalized through a framework comprising three core constituent elements: Purpose, Values, and GAI Properties. This taxonomy, derived from extensive literature analysis, provides a structured vocabulary for discussing and implementing human-centric principles [6].

Purpose defines the fundamental objectives and motivations behind an HCGAI system and encompasses three primary goals. The first is augmentation, which focuses on enhancing human intelligence, skills, and decision-making processes. This is exemplified by decision-support systems where GAI acts as a collaborator, offering insights or generating options for human consideration. The second is GAI autonomy, referring to the system's ability to make decisions and take actions without direct, moment-to-moment human intervention. While autonomy may appear to conflict with human control, it can be highly valuable in contexts requiring rapid action or in collaborative environments where GAI functions as a hybrid team member with complementary strengths. The third is automation, which involves delegating repetitive, mundane, or time-consuming tasks to GAI systems to improve efficiency. Unlike autonomy, which can involve non-deterministic behavior, automation typically operates according to prescriptive rules, providing predictable and consistent task execution.

Values represent the guiding framework of fundamental beliefs and ideals that shape the design and behavior of HCGAI systems, and they can be categorized into three groups. Ethical values focus on ensuring that the technology is developed and deployed in an ethically sound manner, encompassing dignity—respecting the inherent worth of individuals—fairness, which ensures equitable treatment and the absence of bias, and justice, which seeks to distribute GAI's benefits widely while including marginalized groups in the design process. Protection values relate to safeguarding fundamental human rights and well-being, including privacy, which protects personal data; safety, which shields users from harm; and prevention of harm, which proactively mitigates potential risks. Such protection is especially critical when users provide personal information in prompts to GAI models. Performance values aim to maximize the benefits of GAI for both individuals and society, emphasizing efficiency in optimizing resource use, effectiveness in achieving intended goals, and accuracy in delivering correct and precise results.

GAI properties are the specific, verifiable characteristics that a GAI system must possess to be considered trustworthy and human-centric, and they can be divided into three categories. Oversight properties pertain to the ability to monitor, review, and regulate GAI systems, encompassing accountability, which assigns responsibility for GAI actions; controllability, which enables humans to intervene or override the system; responsibility, which reflects the moral duty to consider societal interests; and sustainability, which accounts for long-term environmental and societal impacts. Comprehension properties focus on improving human understanding of GAI systems, including explainability, which makes the system's inner workings understandable; intelligibility, which ensures outputs are presented in a comprehensible manner; and transparency, which provides insight into data sources, algorithms, and intentions. Integrity properties ensure that GAI systems operate consistently and dependably, incorporating reliability for consistent performance, robustness to handle unexpected or adversarial conditions, trustworthiness to remain lawful, ethical, and resilient, and traceability to enable tracking of decision-making processes.

While this framework provides a clear taxonomy, its application in the real world is far from a simple checklist. The core elements of HCGAI exist in a state of inherent tension. For instance, the pursuit of the *purpose* of automation to maximize the *performance value* of efficiency, as seen in automated credit granting, can directly conflict with the *oversight property* of human controllability and may undermine the *ethical value* of dignity if it leads to opaque, unchallengeable decisions [7]. Similarly, the use of GAI in creative industries can dramatically accelerate production timelines (efficiency), but it simultaneously raises difficult questions about authorship, originality (integrity properties), and the potential for job displacement, which challenges the value of human dignity [2]. Achieving full GAI autonomy inherently challenges the properties of comprehension and oversight. Therefore, the practical design of a human-centric system is not about maximizing all these elements simultaneously. Rather, it is an exercise in navigating and balancing these competing concerns in a principled and context-aware manner. The HCGAI framework is best understood not as a set of absolute goals but as a map of potential trade-offs that require careful deliberation, negotiation, and compromise throughout the design process.

4.1.5 Formal Model of HCGAI

Human-Centered Generative AI (HGAI) represents a crucial paradigm shift in the development of artificial intelligence, moving beyond purely technical performance to prioritize human values, needs, and capabilities. At its core, HGAI is defined by a hierarchy of three fundamental objectives: aligning with human values to ensure ethical behavior, assimilating human intents to create a seamless and controllable user experience, and ultimately, augmenting human abilities to act as a collaborative partner in creative and professional domains. This approach is not merely a design philosophy but a necessary framework to address the significant ethical challenges posed by generative technologies, including algorithmic bias, the protection of creators' rights, and the prevention of misuse. By embedding human-centric principles throughout the entire lifecycle—from data collection and model training to final deployment and evaluation—HGAI aims to foster a symbiotic relationship between humans and GAI that is both productive and responsible.

To translate these qualitative principles into a structured and measurable methodology, it is beneficial to construct a formal model. Such a model provides a rigorous framework for optimizing generative systems against the core objectives of HGAI. By defining variables for the GAI, its users, and the guiding principles of values and intents, we can establish quantifiable objective functions and constraints. This formalization allows developers and researchers to systematically evaluate trade-offs, manage risks according to established frameworks like the NIST AI Risk Management Framework, and integrate human factors from the earliest stages of design. The following model synthesizes the conceptual frameworks from the provided research into a unified mathematical structure, offering a clear path for the development and assessment of truly human-centered generative systems. Let us define a formal mathematical model for Human-Centered Generative AI (HGAI), integrating core concepts extracted from the provided documents.

Definitions and Notation

Let:

- G represents the Generative AI model.
- U denotes human users interacting with the AI system.
- D represents the training dataset, comprising human-generated or human-validated data.
- V symbolizes human values embedded within Al behavior.
- I symbolizes human intents conveyed during interactions.
- H represents human capabilities to be augmented by AI.

Objective Functions

The HGAI model comprises three hierarchical objectives.

1. Aligning with Human Values (Level 1): Ensure that generated outputs align with human ethical and cultural values. Formally:

$$\max_G f_{align}(G, V) = E_{x \sim D}\left[\text{AlignmentScore}(G(x), V)\right]$$

   subject to

$$(G(D)) \leq \epsilon, \ \epsilon \geq 0$$

2. Assimilating Human Intents (Level 2): Facilitate effective assimilation and responsiveness to human intents, enabling clear and iterative refinement of AI-generated outputs:

$$\max_G f_{\text{intent}}(G, I) = E_{u \sim U}[\text{IntentAssimilationScore}(G(u), I)]$$

subject to

$$\text{Deviation}(G(u), I) \leq \delta, \delta \geq 0$$

3. Augmenting Human Abilities (Level 3): Enhance human performance through cooperative interactions, improving task efficacy:

$$\max_{G} f_{\text{augment}}(G, H) = E_{u\sim U}\left[\text{AugmentationScore}(G(u), H)\right]$$

subject to

$$(G(u), H) \geq \gamma, \gamma > 0$$

Integrated Optimization

A unified objective function combining the above three levels using weighted sums can be represented as

$$\max_{G} F(G) = \alpha f_{\text{align}}(G, V) + \beta f_{\text{intent}}(G, I) + \zeta f_{\text{augment}}(G, H)$$

where α, β, ζ are weighting coefficients satisfying:

$$\alpha + \beta + \zeta = 1, \alpha, \beta, \zeta \geq 0$$

Constraints and Risk Management

Using the NIST AI Risk Management Framework, let the AI Risk function $R(G)$ be defined as

$$R(G) = \text{MAP}(G) + \text{MEASURE}(G) + \text{MANAGE}(G) + \text{GOVERN}(G)$$

subject to

$$R(G) \leq R_{\max}, R_{\max} \geq 0$$

Human-Centered Generative Design (HCGD) Integration

To ensure early design integration, let the conceptual generative design function $C(G, U)$ be

$$\max_{C} f_{\text{concept}}(C, U) = E_{u\sim U}\left[\text{ConceptEval}(C(u), G)\right]$$

subject to

$$\text{HumanFactors}(C(u), G) \geq \theta, \theta > 0$$

Solution Space

The feasible solution space S for the HGAI optimization problem is

$$S = \left\{G | f_{\text{align}}, f_{\text{intent}}, f_{\text{augment}}, f_{\text{concept}} \text{ satisfy all constraints above}\right\}$$

This formal mathematical model integrates human values, intents, and capabilities into Generative AI frameworks, providing a structured approach to developing ethical, effective, and human-centered generative systems.

4.2 A Triptych of Design Philosophies

Operationalizing the principles of HCGAI requires concrete methodologies that can guide the design and development process from conception to implementation. Three cornerstone philosophies have emerged as central to this effort: Participatory and Co-Design, Value-Sensitive Design (VSD), and Human-in-the-Loop (HITL). While distinct in their primary focus, these approaches are increasingly understood as complementary components of a holistic strategy for creating responsible and effective GAI. This section provides a deep, comparative analysis of each philosophy, examining its core tenets, practical applications, and inherent challenges.

4.2.1 Participatory and Co-design: Empowering Stakeholders

Participatory design is a collaborative approach that fundamentally repositions the role of end-users and other stakeholders, transforming them from passive subjects of study into active partners in the design process [8]. This methodology is particularly crucial for GAI development, where a disconnect between the technical capabilities of a system and the real-world needs, values, and contexts of its users can lead to tools that are ineffective, irrelevant, or even harmful [9]. By involving stakeholders directly in activities like ideation, prototyping, and evaluation, co-design aims to bridge this gap, ensuring that the resulting technology is grounded in lived experience [8].

A powerful demonstration of this approach is the "La Independiente" platform, a suite of AI-enhanced tools co-designed with and for Latin American crowd-workers [10]. The project began with surveys and participatory design sessions to address a significant knowledge gap regarding the needs of this workforce, particularly women [10]. This direct engagement revealed that beyond simple task efficiency, workers valued community, culturally relevant self-representation, and support for language barriers. In response, the co-designed platform included features like a conversational assistant for job matching, a recommendation system for sharing peer experiences, and an AI-powered plugin to generate culturally resonant professional biographies [10]. The project's success underscores how participatory methods can lead to the creation of tools that are not only functionally useful but also deeply meaningful and empowering for their target community. So, "La Independiente" platform is the best example of GAI designed and developed with a participatory approach.

The application of co-design extends to refining interactions with general-purpose AI systems. For example, one study engaged qualitative researchers in co-design sessions to develop a framework for crafting better prompts for ChatGPT, ultimately improving its utility for qualitative analysis [11]. By involving the experts who would use the tool, the research moved beyond generic prompt engineering to create guidance tailored to a specific professional practice. A similar ethos drives the "Matchmaking for GAI" framework, which uses abstracted "GAI Probes" to help non-experts, such as professional fact-checkers, understand NLP capabilities and collaboratively design tools with GAI researchers that meet their specific workflow needs [12].

Despite its benefits, participatory design of GAI is not without challenges. The very act of introducing GAI into the process can create new barriers to entry. Even as GAI tools may lower the threshold for participation by, for instance, helping users visualize ideas, they may simultaneously introduce a new requirement for "GAI literacy," potentially excluding those unfamiliar with how to effectively interact with these systems [8].

Addressing this tension requires deliberate strategies to bridge the gap between accessibility and capability. This involves not only designing intuitive interfaces and interaction models but also fostering inclusive education and training initiatives that demystify GAI for diverse user groups. By empowering participants with the knowledge and confidence to engage meaningfully, designers can ensure that the benefits of participatory GAI are equitably distributed, mitigating the risk of reinforcing existing digital divides and fostering a more genuinely collaborative innovation ecosystem.

4.2.2 *Value-Sensitive Design (VSD): Proactively Embedding Ethics*

While participatory design focuses on the "who" and "how" of collaboration, Value-Sensitive Design (VSD) provides a systematic methodology for addressing the "what"—the human values that a technology should embody [13]. VSD is a principled approach that seeks to proactively account for human values throughout the entire design process, rather than treating ethical considerations as an afterthought or a post-deployment patch [13].

The methodology is structured around a three-part, iterative investigation [13]. The first phase, conceptual investigation, focuses on identifying the direct and indirect stakeholders of a technology and eliciting the values that are central to their context. This stage involves clarifying these values and examining potential conflicts that might arise from the technology's use, such as tensions between convenience and privacy. The second phase, empirical investigation, uses social science methods to explore how stakeholders experience and prioritize the identified values in practice, aiming to understand human responses to the technology within its broader context of use. The third phase, technical investigation, centers on designing the system to support the values uncovered in the conceptual and empirical stages. This may involve analyzing how existing technologies support or hinder certain values, or proactively developing new systems with features specifically designed to uphold these values.

In the context of GAI, VSD has been adapted to address the specific challenges of machine learning systems, such as their opacity and potential for emergent, unintended behaviors [14]. The "black box" nature of many GAI models makes it crucial to prioritize values like transparency, explainability, and accountability from the outset [14]. To this end, researchers have proposed extending the VSD process to encompass the entire GAI lifecycle, allowing for continuous monitoring and redesign as unintended value consequences emerge over time [15]. This lifecycle approach is critical for GAI, whose adaptive nature can cause it to drift away from its initially embedded values. A related approach, Value-Sensitive Algorithm Design (VSAD), specifically emphasizes engaging stakeholders in the earliest stages of algorithm creation to avoid embedding biases in core design choices [16].

Integrating VSD and VSAD within GAI development thus calls for a proactive, iterative methodology that not only embeds stakeholder values at inception but also revisits and refines these alignments as the system evolves. This continuous engagement fosters a feedback loop where human perspectives guide algorithmic adaptation, ensuring that emerging functionalities remain consistent with ethical commitments. Such an approach recognizes that in the dynamic landscape of GAI, safeguarding human values is not a one-time design decision but an ongoing responsibility embedded in the technology's operational fabric.

4.2.3 *Human-in-the-Loop (HITL): Integrating Human Judgment*

Human-in-the-Loop (HITL) is a design philosophy that operationalizes human oversight by creating a symbiotic collaboration between humans and GAI systems [17]. It reframes automation not as a complete replacement of human effort, but as a human–computer interaction problem [18]. The core premise is that while GAI excels at processing vast amounts of data and identifying patterns, humans possess superior capabilities in areas requiring nuanced judgment, contextual understanding, ethical reasoning, and handling of ambiguous or incomplete information [7].

HITL integrates human expertise at various stages of the GAI lifecycle [17]. Human involvement in GAI systems occurs at multiple stages of the development and deployment lifecycle. During training, humans provide high-quality labels for the training data, a process that can be enhanced through active learning, where the model selectively queries humans for labels on the most informative data points. During evaluation, humans play a critical role in assessing model performance and offering feedback on predictions to identify areas for improvement—an especially important step for generative models, where automated metrics often fall short in capturing the quality or appropriateness of the outputs. During operation, humans remain in the decision-making loop to supervise, guide, or override the actions of the GAI, which is particularly vital in high-stakes domains where mistakes could lead to severe consequences.

Case studies demonstrate the broad applicability of the HITL approach. In finance, human experts are involved in reviewing GAI-driven assessments of creditworthiness to ensure fairness and account for individual circumstances [7]. In content moderation, humans make final judgments on nuanced cases that automated systems flag. In banking, HITL is used to manage complex Know Your Customer (KYC) onboarding processes, and in healthcare, it supports the management of insurance claim denials [19]. The feasibility of a HITL approach has also been demonstrated for creating complex educational assessments at scale, where human review ensures the quality of GAI-generated content [20].

However, the HITL approach is not a universal solution for GAI risk. The human in the loop can be a source of error or bias themselves. For example, in the process of Reinforcement Learning from Human Feedback (RLHF), the biases of the human labelers can be encoded into the model, potentially reinforcing societal inequities [21]. Therefore, a successful HITL system requires careful design of the human–machine interaction to mitigate these risks and ensure that human involvement is both meaningful and effective [7].

The examination of these three design philosophies reveals that they are not isolated, competing methodologies but are, in fact, converging into integrated, hybrid frameworks. The most effective and responsible approaches to designing human-centric GAI do not choose one philosophy over the others but weave them together into a cohesive strategy. The process starts with the recognition that these are complementary tools for solving different aspects of the same core problem. A project might begin with Participatory Design methods, such as co-design workshops, to engage directly with stakeholders. The primary goal of this initial phase is to elicit their needs, contexts, and, crucially, their Values—the central concern of VSD. Once a key value like "fairness" or "user agency" is identified and prioritized, this informs the technical design. This is where HITL becomes a critical implementation strategy. The VSD requirement for "human control" or "accountability" is operationalized by designing a HITL mechanism, such as a review stage for potentially biased outputs or an interface that gives users explicit control over the generative process.

This convergence is evident in practice. The "La Independiente" project, while rooted in co-design, was explicitly aimed at creating tools that reflected the *values* of its users, a VSD principle [10]. The comprehensive frameworks for responsible GAI, which are extensions of VSD, explicitly call for Human Oversight and Control as a core property, which is the functional domain of HITL [15]. This methodological synthesis demonstrates a maturation of the field, moving from the advocacy of distinct philosophies to the development of an integrated, pragmatic toolkit for building genuinely human-centric systems.

4.2.4 Synthesis and Comparison

To clarify the distinct contributions and complementary nature of these philosophies, the following table provides a comparative analysis (Table 4.1).

Table 4.1 Comparative analysis of core design methodologies

Methodology	Primary goal	Key stakeholders	Core activities	Primary output	Key challenge
Participatory/ co-design	To create useful and relevant systems by empowering users as active design partners	End-users, community members, domain experts	Co-design workshops, participatory prototyping, user-led needs analysis	A system that is grounded in the lived experiences and practical needs of its users	Scaling deep, qualitative engagement to match rapid development cycles
Value-sensitive design (VSD)	To proactively embed human values (e.g., privacy, fairness, accountability) into technology	All direct and indirect stakeholders, including society at large	Conceptual, Empirical, and Technical investigations of values	A system whose architecture and features are explicitly aligned with identified ethical and social values	Translating abstract values into concrete, verifiable technical requirements
Human-in-the-loop (HITL)	To improve system performance and ensure safety by integrating human judgment and oversight	Domain experts, human labelers, system supervisors	Data labeling, model evaluation, real-time decision oversight, feedback provision (RLHF)	A hybrid human-GAI system that combines computational power with human intelligence for greater accuracy and reliability	Designing effective human-GAI interaction and mitigating the introduction of human bias

4.2.5 Unified Design and Development Pipeline for Human-Centric Generative AI

The integration of design and development is an essential component of effectively integrating human-centric values into generative AI systems. Ethical considerations, user feedback, and governance structures need not necessarily be viewed as isolated components; rather, we view them as interconnected through a systematic framework that underpins the process of designing and developing these systems as a whole. As a result, it enables the implementation of human needs, cultural contexts, and expectations directly into the design and into all phases of the system's lifecycle, including development, deployment, and post-deployment.

By focusing on developing engineering-based methodologies for converting the high-level philosophical concepts of human-centric design to practical representations of the intended operational characteristics of the system, the approach allows the possibility of directly linking human and cultural needs to an effective implementation of a generative AI solution. The first step of this process is to identify and define the human values that are relevant to our business, followed by engaging stakeholder representatives in participatory design activities that result in their input on what "human-centric" means for their business. Once this input has been gathered, we will take that input and create technical bounding constraints and objectives that allow us to construct a generative model that is operating within very clearly defined human-aligned boundaries. The ongoing human oversight and feedback on the system will help ensure that it continues to operate consistently, maintain a high level of trust, and evolve over time in a manner that is responsive and adaptable.

As shown in Fig. 4.1, the design and development pipeline illustrates the chronological flow from "human value" input through to "Participatory Input" and finally "value-sensitive design mapping" through to "Human in the Loop" during development of the generative model.

To further operationalize the proposed pipeline, Table 4.2 presents a stage-wise mapping of human-centric design philosophies to key phases of generative AI development.

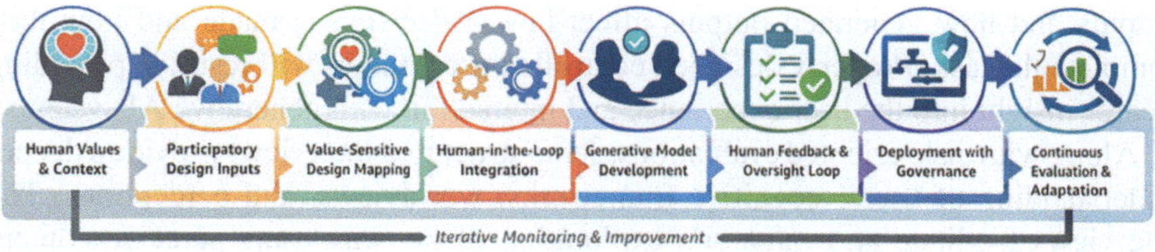

Fig. 4.1 HC-GAI unified design and development pipeline integrating human values, participatory inputs, value-sensitive design, and human-in-the-loop mechanisms across the generative AI lifecycle

Table 4.2 Demonstrates how major human-centric design philosophies align with different stages of generative AI development

Development stage	Participatory design	Value-sensitive design	Human-in-the-loop
Problem definition	Stakeholder workshops	Identification of core human values	Expert validation
Data collection	User-informed data selection	Bias-aware dataset curation	Human review
Model training	User requirements feedback	Ethical constraint integration	Manual checkpoints
Generation phase	User interaction design	Value-aligned output control	Output approval
Deployment	User onboarding	Compliance monitoring	Override mechanisms

This structured mapping provides a clear methodology for translating abstract ethical and human-centered principles into concrete system design and development workflows

4.2.6 *Evaluation in Practice*

A multidimensional evaluation framework for human-centric generative artificial intelligence systems should be used with an evaluation involving human stakeholders throughout all phases of the evaluation process instead of solely relying on complete computer-automated evaluations. The automated metrics will give general indicators of baseline performance but will not adequately measure many of the human-centered metrics of these systems (e.g., trust, usability, interpretability, and perceived fairness). As such, the use of human judgment, qualitative observations, and contextual feedback will be necessary for the evaluation of the effect of a generative AI system in addition to using quantitative performance metrics. One effective way to evaluate generative AIs in practice is through controlled user studies by having participants perform representative tasks on the generative AI system under controlled conditions. A controlled user study will yield quantitative performance metrics such as time to complete task, errors, and efficiency of interactions, as well as the incentives and qualitative observations of participant experiences in interacting with generated outputs and how generated outputs affect how a decision is made and how they complete the task. Properly designed controlled user studies will result in providing clearer insight into the user experience and interaction with generative AI systems.

Along with task-oriented evaluations, semi-structured interviews provide a deeper understanding of users' cognitive frameworks, worldviews, and perceptions. The interviews facilitate an evaluator's exploration of the way users perceive content created by the system, how much they trust the system, and whether or not they recognize the possible constraints and ambiguity involved with generative output. This type of qualitative data will often reveal discrepancies between what the system's designers intended and how users interpret or experience the system's functionality, particularly if those differences are not recognized through quantitative measurement alone. Surveys and standard questionnaires provide additional opportunities for practical evaluations through the systematic measuring of subjective concepts. Commonly accepted evaluation instruments such as the System Usability Scale (SUS), trust questionnaires, and perceived usefulness scales can be used to measure the usability, satisfaction, and confidence a user has in the system. Administering these instruments to a wide variety of users allows for the identification of differences in the way people experience the system based on the individuals' level of expertise, background, or task context and provides a stronger foundation for creating inclusive, human-centered design of systems. Continuous evaluation of deployed generative AI systems is necessary. Lightweight feedback tools, such as thumbs up/down, rating scales, or brief feedback forms included within the user interface, allow for the collection of large numbers of real-world user reactions over time.

This form of in-situ evaluation enables the detection of emergent issues, such as unexpected biases, misleading outputs, or declining user trust over time. Importantly, such feedback supports iterative refinement, allowing developers to adapt models and interfaces in response to evolving user needs and usage patterns.

Expert evaluation is extremely important in the application of generative AI for high-stakes or socially sensitive applications (systems and use of generative AI). Domain expertise, ethics, and auditing are used by experts to assess compliance with regulations and also evaluate the ethical use of a system and its ability to correctly perform a domain-specific task. While end users can usually identify the majority of risks/losses within a system, expert review will typically be able to identify latent risks that may not be readily apparent to others, such as subtle or complex biases or harmful content generation or misalignment of the system with organizational/social values. Also, the idea that evaluation is not a one-time assessment but rather a process throughout the lifecycle of a system is a critical component of practical evaluation ("practical") of a system. Both longitudinal evaluations are essential to monitoring the evolution of human/user trust and interaction patterns with the system and ensuring that the system remains aligned with human-centered goals. As such, ethical considerations are also very important in the practical evaluation of a system. Researchers must obtain informed consent for human-subject studies, be transparent regarding the system capabilities, and ensure the protection of user data and privacy as outlined by established ethical standards. Participants should be made aware of the generative nature of the system and any potential limitations or risks associated with its use. Embedding ethical safeguards within the evaluation process itself reinforces the broader human-centric philosophy guiding system development.

4.3 From Blueprint to Reality: The Development Lifecycle

Transitioning from high-level design philosophies to tangible, functional systems require a focus on the practicalities of implementation. This involves crafting intuitive user interfaces that foster effective human-GAI collaboration and adopting operational frameworks that can manage the complexity of developing, deploying, and maintaining these systems at scale. This part of the report examines the crucial bridge between the "what" of human-centric principles and the "how" of their realization in software, exploring both the micro-level of interaction design and the macro-level of development methodologies like Agile and GenAIOps.

4.3.1 Designing the Human-GAI Interface: Fostering Effective Collaboration

The user interface (UI) is the critical juncture where human and machine meet. In the context of GAI, the UI is not merely a passive window onto the system's output but an active space for collaboration, control, and negotiation. The design of this interface profoundly shapes the user's experience, their ability to achieve their goals, and their trust in the system. An effective human-centric interface must be designed to manage the unique characteristics of generative technology, including its reliance on user input and its inherently variable and imperfect nature.

4.3.2 The Art and Science of Prompt Engineering

Unlike many traditional software applications, the output quality of a large language model (LLM) or text-to-image model is significantly influenced by the quality of the instructions—the "prompt"—provided by the user [22]. This has given rise to the discipline of prompt engineering, which focuses on crafting inputs that elicit the most desirable and accurate responses from the model. However, effective prompting is a significant challenge for many users [22].

Research indicates that the ability of users to interact effectively with models like ChatGPT is significantly enhanced by three key factors: improving the transparency of the system, providing clear guidance on how to formulate prompts, and strengthening the user's understanding of the LLM's capabilities and limitations [11]. Studies have shown that when users gain familiarity with a model's capabilities and are equipped with effective prompt engineering techniques, their perception of the GAI's role can shift from negative to positive, fostering greater trust and more productive collaboration [11]. Furthermore, while natural language prompts are intuitive, they can also be ambiguous. To address this, researchers are exploring ways to augment text-based instructions with other interaction modalities, such as direct manipulation of generated content, which can allow for more precise and effective expression of human intent [23].

By combining these strategies, GAI systems can move toward more symbiotic forms of interaction, where human and machine contributions complement each other in a fluid, iterative process. Multimodal interfaces, for example, can bridge gaps in understanding by enabling users to refine outputs visually, structurally, or contextually, rather than relying solely on textual instructions. Such enhancements not only reduce ambiguity but also empower users to exert greater creative and strategic control, ultimately fostering a collaborative environment in which human intent is more accurately captured and effectively realized.

4.3.3 Managing Generative Variability

A defining characteristic of GAI is its probabilistic nature. For a single input, a model can produce multiple, distinct outputs, a phenomenon termed "generative variability" [24]. This variability can be a source of creativity and inspiration, but it also presents a design challenge. Users need tools to manage this multiplicity of outputs effectively. Based on the design principles proposed by Weisz et al., this involves several key considerations [24].

Designing for multiple outputs involves creating interfaces that go beyond presenting a single "best" result, instead enabling users to explore a range of possibilities. This includes mechanisms for versioning, where users can save and revisit previous sets of outputs along with the parameters that generated them; curation tools that allow filtering, sorting, and organizing outputs into meaningful collections; annotation features to mark or comment on specific outputs or elements within them; and visualization capabilities to compare multiple outputs, highlighting similarities and differences to help users better understand the design space. Equally important is designing for imperfection, as generative models are not infallible and may produce outputs with factual errors, logical inconsistencies, visual artifacts, subtle biases, or simply results that do not meet the user's subjective needs. A human-centric interface must acknowledge these limitations and provide tools to manage them. This can include evaluation and identification features, such as confidence scores or flags to indicate areas that may require human review; co-creation capabilities that support collaborative workflows where both human and GAI can iteratively edit and refine artifacts; and sandboxing environments that allow users to experiment with generated content safely, ensuring that imperfect outputs are not unintentionally incorporated into production systems.

4.3.4 Affording Human Control and Exploration

To move from being a passive recipient of GAI outputs to an active collaborator, the user must be afforded meaningful control over the generative process. This control is essential for fostering a sense of agency, improving comprehension, and enabling exploration of the vast space of potential outputs [24].

Effective controls in generative AI can be understood across three distinct levels. Generic controls apply broadly across different generative technologies and domains, such as the "temperature" parameter, which allows users to adjust the degree of randomness or "creativity" in the output, balancing diversity with coherence, or the option to set the number of outputs generated per request. Technology-specific controls are linked to the underlying GAI architecture; for instance, in GANs, users might manipulate the latent space to modify the semantic attributes of an image, while in LLMs, the focus is on prompt engineering to influence the style, structure, or content of the generated text. Domain-specific controls are tailored to the nature of the artifact being created. In generative engineering design, this could mean defining material constraints or performance objectives, whereas in text generation, it might involve specifying a target reading level or tone to suit the intended audience. By providing a rich set of controls, the interface encourages users to interactively explore the model's capabilities, helping them build a more accurate mental model of how the system works and what it can achieve [24].

When thoughtfully integrated, these layered controls transform the user's role from that of a mere consumer to an engaged co-creator, fostering a deeper understanding of the interplay between human input and machine output. Such interaction not only enhances creative exploration but also supports iterative refinement, where users can progressively steer the generative process toward their intended vision. Over time, this active engagement cultivates both technical fluency and critical awareness, enabling users to harness GAI as a versatile partner in problem-solving, innovation, and artistic expression.

4.3.5 Building Trust Through Interaction

The design of the human-GAI interface is not just a matter of technical functionality; it is a critical site where ethical principles are either upheld or undermined. The interface is the primary mechanism through which values like transparency, agency, and accountability are operationalized for the end-user. The choices a designer makes about what controls to expose, how system imperfections are framed, and how much transparency is provided directly shape the user's ability to act as a responsible and empowered collaborator.

For example, an interface that hides the "temperature" control or other parameters limits the user's agency and their ability to tailor the output to their specific needs. An interface that does not facilitate the easy comparison of multiple outputs makes it more difficult for a user to spot subtle biases or inconsistencies. As research has shown, improving transparency and providing clear guidance on interaction can directly foster user trust and lead to a more positive and productive perception of the GAI's role [11]. Clearly communicating the GAI's intended role—be it an assistant, a coach, or a creative partner—and being upfront about its limitations helps users calibrate their expectations and trust appropriately [24]. Ultimately, a human-centric interface is one that treats the user as an intelligent agent, providing them with the tools and information necessary to guide the GAI, evaluate its output critically, and take ultimate responsibility for the final product.

Such an approach not only empowers users to make informed choices but also reinforces the collaborative nature of human–GAI interactions. By framing the system as a partner whose outputs are subject to human judgment and refinement, the interface encourages active engagement rather than passive acceptance. This dynamic approach fosters a culture of shared responsibility, where human oversight and machine capability work in tandem to produce outcomes that are not only technically robust but also aligned with the user's values, goals, and contextual constraints.

4.4 Operationalizing Intelligence at Scale: Agile and GenAIOps

While interaction design focuses on the individual user's experience, building and maintaining robust GAI systems for widespread use requires a disciplined, scalable approach to the entire software development lifecycle. This has led to the adaptation of established methodologies like Agile and the creation of new, specialized operational frameworks like GenAIOps. These approaches aim to manage the unique complexities of GAI development, ensuring that systems can be built, deployed, and updated efficiently, reliably, and responsibly.

4.4.1 Adapting Agile for the Age of GAI

The Agile methodology, with its emphasis on iterative development, rapid response to change, and continuous stakeholder feedback, is well-suited to the experimental nature of GAI development [25]. Generative AI, in turn, can act as a powerful "force multiplier" for Agile teams. By automating or accelerating tasks like boilerplate code generation, unit test creation, user story breakdown, and documentation, GAI can significantly shorten development cycles and feedback loops [25]. This allows teams to iterate more quickly and focus human effort on higher-value activities like complex problem-solving, architectural design, and strategic planning [26].

However, the integration of GAI into Agile workflows is not without its challenges. The very speed it enables can introduce risks if not managed carefully. For instance, one report found that a 25% increase in GAI adoption correlated with a drop in both delivery throughput and stability, suggesting that the rapid generation of code can lead to new complexities and integration issues if not properly tested and reviewed [27]. This highlights the critical importance of maintaining a human-in-the-loop mindset within the development team. GAI should be treated as a "junior teammate" or a "cybernetic collaborator"—fast and helpful, but whose work requires rigorous oversight and validation by experienced human developers [25].

Successfully adapting Agile for the GAI era requires several shifts in practice. Teams must move beyond simply measuring output-based metrics like velocity and focus more on outcome-focused measures like cycle time and lead time, where learning and experimentation are treated as valuable deliverables [28]. Clear governance is needed to define which tasks are suitable for GAI assistance and where human judgment is non-negotiable [25]. This creates a dynamic tension between the desire for agility and the need for robust governance. While GAI can accelerate the coding phase of an Agile sprint, the operational overhead of managing the complex systems that power it introduces new forms of friction. This "Agile-Governance" paradox means that the most mature teams will be those that successfully integrate the necessary checks and balances of AI governance into their iterative workflows, forging a new discipline of "Governed Agility."

In practice, achieving Governed Agility demands that teams embed governance mechanisms directly into their development pipelines, ensuring compliance and ethical alignment without stifling innovation. This can involve automated validation checks, bias detection tools, and traceability mechanisms that operate alongside traditional Agile ceremonies. By treating governance as an enabler rather than a constraint, teams can maintain rapid iteration cycles while safeguarding against the risks inherent in GAI deployment, ultimately fostering a development culture that is both fast-moving and responsibly grounded.

4.4.2 MLOps: The Foundation for Production GAI

As machine learning models moved from research labs into production environments, the need for a more disciplined approach to their lifecycle became apparent. Machine Learning Operations (MLOps) emerged to fill this gap, applying the principles of DevOps—such as continuous integration and continuous delivery (CI/CD), automation, and version control—to the unique challenges of machine learning [29].

MLOps provides a framework for managing the end-to-end lifecycle of ML models, from data ingestion and pre-processing to model training, validation, deployment, and monitoring [30]. Key practices include version control, which involves tracking changes not only in code but also in datasets and models to ensure reproducibility and auditability. Automation plays a critical role by streamlining the ML pipeline—covering data processing, model training, and deployment—to guarantee consistency, scalability, and repeatability. Continuous monitoring is equally important, enabling the detection of issues such as data drift or performance degradation in production environments, which can then trigger automated retraining and redeployment to maintain optimal system performance. By standardizing these processes, MLOps enables organizations to deploy and maintain ML models more efficiently, reliably, and at scale [31].

In the context of GAI, these MLOps principles evolve into GenAIOps, which extends the framework to address the additional complexity of managing generative models and their supporting application stacks. This includes handling unstructured and multimodal data, integrating retrieval-augmented generation pipelines, and governing prompt engineering workflows. Moreover, GenAIOps must account for unique operational concerns such as evaluating creative outputs, ensuring content safety, and managing computational costs associated with large-scale generation. By building on MLOps foundations while incorporating these domain-specific requirements, GenAIOps provides a robust operational backbone for delivering generative AI solutions that are scalable, trustworthy, and aligned with organizational goals.

4.4.3 GenAIOps: Extending MLOps for Generative AI

Traditional MLOps provides a strong foundation, but the unique nature of GAI workloads requires an extension of these practices, a field now known as Generative AI Operations (GenAIOps) or LLMOps [32]. Generative AI solutions differ from traditional ML in that the focus often shifts from training a model from scratch to consuming, fine-tuning, and extending large foundation models [33].

The key asset in a GenAI system is often not just the model itself, but the entire application stack that surrounds it. This includes new technical patterns that must be managed within the operational lifecycle, such as prompt engineering, where the prompts and prompt templates used to interact with the model are critical assets that need to be versioned, tested, and evaluated. Another important pattern is retrieval-augmented generation (RAG), in which the model's knowledge is supplemented with information retrieved from external data stores, such as vector databases. This approach introduces additional components—such as the orchestrator that manages the logic, the data ingestion pipelines, and the vector indexes—that must be governed within the operational framework.

This necessitates extending the MLOps lifecycle across several key stages. DataOps must be expanded to handle the processing of unstructured documents for RAG, incorporating strategies for document chunking, data enrichment, embedding generation, and the maintenance of vector search indexes. Experimentation broadens beyond tuning model hyperparameters to include tracking variations in chunking strategies, embedding models, prompt designs, and search configurations. Evaluation also requires specialized metrics-RAG systems, for instance, demand measures of groundedness (whether the response is based on the provided context), relevancy (whether the response answers the user's query), and completeness. For other generative tasks, metrics like BLEU and ROUGE may still be applied but need to be supplemented with human evaluation. Deployment extends beyond the model to encompass the orchestrator and other application components, while monitoring must address new concerns such as retrieval system performance, the quality of generated responses, token usage for cost management, and content safety to identify and moderate harmful outputs. Overall, GenAIOps represents a significant increase in operational complexity compared to traditional MLOps, requiring new tooling, specialized expertise, and a holistic view of the AI application as an integrated system of models, data, and code.

4.5 Evaluating and Safeguarding Human-GAI Systems

The development of effective and responsible GAI does not end with deployment. The probabilistic, adaptive, and often opaque nature of these systems demands continuous evaluation and proactive safeguarding. This part of the report addresses two of the most critical challenges in the field: first, how to measure the success of a human-centric system in a way that captures the nuances of human-GAI collaboration, and second, how to confront and mitigate the pervasive risks of bias and unfairness that can be amplified by these powerful technologies.

4.5.1 Measuring What Matters: A Multidimensional Evaluation Framework

Evaluating the performance of GAI systems is a complex endeavor. While traditional automated metrics from fields like Natural Language Processing (NLP) and Computer Vision (CV) provide a starting point, they are fundamentally insufficient for capturing the qualities that matter most in a human-centric context. A truly meaningful evaluation must move beyond measuring technical correctness to assess the quality of the generated output, the effectiveness of the user experience, and the trustworthiness of the system as a whole.

4.5.2 The Limitations of Automated Metrics

For tasks like machine translation or text summarization, automated metrics such as BLEU (Bilingual Evaluation Understudy), ROUGE (Recall-Oriented Understudy for Gisting Evaluation), and BERTScore have long been standard [33]. These metrics work by comparing a machine-generated output to one or more human-created reference outputs, measuring lexical or semantic overlap. While useful for benchmarking and during development, they have significant limitations. They often fail to capture subjective but critical qualities like creativity, contextual appropriateness, factual accuracy, coherence, and nuance [34]. A response can achieve a high BLEU score while being grammatically awkward, logically flawed, or subtly misleading. For generative tasks, where there is no single "correct" answer, these metrics are even less adequate.

4.5.3 A Taxonomy of Human-Centered Evaluation

To address these shortcomings, a multidimensional evaluation framework grounded in human judgment is required. By synthesizing metrics discussed across a wide range of recent research, we can construct a comprehensive taxonomy for evaluating human-centric GAI. This taxonomy is organized around three key dimensions: the quality of the output, the quality of the user's interaction, and the integrity of the system [34].

1. **Output Quality Metrics**: These metrics assess the generated artifact itself, relying on human evaluators to judge its intrinsic qualities.
   - ***Fluency and Coherence***: Does the output use grammatically correct, natural, and readable language? Does it maintain a logical flow and thematic consistency [34]?
   - ***Accuracy and Relevance***: How well does the output reflect factual reality or the intended meaning? Does the content align with the user's intent and the given context [34]?
   - ***Human-Likeness and Creativity***: Does the output exhibit qualities associated with human expression, such as empathy, appropriate emotional nuance, or originality? For creative content, evaluators can assess novelty and adherence to a desired style [34].
2. **Usability and Experience Metrics**: These metrics focus on the user's interaction with the GAI system, assessing how effectively and satisfactorily they can use it to achieve their goals.
   - ***Ease of Use and Task Success Rate***: How intuitive and straightforward is the system to operate? Can users successfully complete their intended tasks using the GAI [34]?
   - ***Helpfulness***: Does the GAI provide valuable assistance that genuinely meets the user's needs? This is particularly relevant for conversational agents and support tools [34].
   - ***User Satisfaction and Overall Experience***: How do users rate their overall interaction? This measures general satisfaction, engagement, and even enjoyment derived from using the system [34].
3. **Trust and Transparency Metrics**: These metrics evaluate the system's integrity and the user's ability to comprehend and trust its operations.
   - ***Interpretability and Explainability***: Are the GAI's decisions and outputs understandable to non-experts? Can users comprehend the reasoning behind a particular response [34]?
   - ***Trust and Confidence***: Do users feel confident in the GAI's reliability? Do they trust the information it provides? This is often a result of consistent performance, transparency, and perceived fairness [6].

- ***Fairness***: Does the system produce equitable outcomes across different user groups? This involves human assessment of potential biases and stereotypes in the output.

4.5.4 Evaluation in Practice

Implementing this multidimensional framework requires moving beyond automated scripts to actively involve human evaluators. This can be achieved through controlled user studies, where participants perform tasks with the GAI system, enabling the collection of both quantitative data—such as task completion time and error rates—and qualitative feedback. Semi-structured interviews further provide rich insights into users' perceptions, mental models, and overall experiences. Surveys and standardized questionnaires, such as the System Usability Scale, can be employed to measure subjective constructs like usability, user satisfaction, and trust. For deployed systems, continuous feedback mechanisms, including simple tools like "thumbs up/down" buttons or short feedback forms, allow for large-scale collection of real-world evaluation data. Such feedback is invaluable for detecting emergent issues and driving ongoing improvements.

4.5.5 An Integrated Evaluation Model

To provide a clear, actionable guide for practitioners, these diverse metrics can be organized into an integrated model. This model helps teams think about evaluation holistically, ensuring that all critical dimensions of a human-centric system are considered (Table 4.3).

4.6 Confronting Inequity: Bias and Fairness in Generative Systems

Perhaps the most significant ethical challenge facing GAI is the problem of bias. Because these models learn from vast datasets that reflect existing societal inequities, they can inadvertently learn, reproduce, and even amplify harmful stereotypes and discriminatory patterns. Ensuring fairness in generative systems is a complex, multifaceted problem that requires a proactive and multi-pronged approach, spanning from the data used for training to the algorithms themselves and the final outputs they produce.

Table 4.3 A multidimensional framework for evaluating human-centric GAI

Evaluation dimension	Metric category	Specific metric	Description	Example application
Generated output quality	Linguistic quality	Fluency, coherence	Assesses grammatical correctness, readability, and logical flow	Evaluating a text summarization model to ensure the summary is well-written and easy to follow
	Semantic quality	Accuracy, relevance	Measures factual correctness and alignment with user intent and context	Checking if a RAG-based chatbot's answer is factually correct and directly addresses the user's question
	Creative quality	Originality, style adherence	Evaluates novelty and conformity to a specified creative style	Assessing if an GAI-generated image successfully captures the "style of Van Gogh" as prompted
User interaction and experience	Usability	Ease of use, task success rate	Measures how intuitive the system is and if users can achieve their goals	Observing users as they try to generate and refine a piece of code with a GAI programming assistant
	Utility	Helpfulness, usefulness	Assesses whether the GAI provides valuable assistance that meets user needs	Surveying users of a healthcare chatbot to determine if its advice was helpful in managing their condition
	Affective quality	User satisfaction, engagement	Measures the user's overall satisfaction and enjoyment from the interaction	Asking users to rate their experience after a conversation with a customer service bot
System trustworthiness and ethics	Comprehensibility	Explainability, transparency	Assesses if users can understand the GAI's reasoning and how it works	Evaluating whether a GAI's natural language explanation of a loan denial decision is clear to the applicant

(continued)

Table 4.3 (continued)

Evaluation dimension	Metric category	Specific metric	Description	Example application
	Reliability	Trust, confidence, consistency	Measures the user's belief in the system's dependability over time	Tracking user trust scores over several interactions to see if they remain high
	Ethical integrity	Fairness, bias detection	Assesses the equity of outcomes and the absence of harmful stereotypes	Having diverse human evaluators review AI-generated images of "a doctor" to check for gender or racial bias

4.6.1 Sources and Manifestations of Bias

Bias in GAI systems is not a monolithic problem; it can originate from multiple sources and manifest in diverse ways. Key sources include

- **Data Bias**: This is the most common source. If the training data is not representative of the real world or contains historical biases, the model will learn these biases. For example, medical imaging datasets that predominantly feature one demographic group can lead to models with reduced accuracy for underrepresented groups [35]. Similarly, text and image data from the internet are rife with gender, racial, and cultural stereotypes, which models readily absorb [36].
- **Algorithmic Bias**: The design of the algorithm itself can introduce bias. This can occur through the choice of optimization function, regularization techniques, or other architectural decisions that may unintentionally favor certain outcomes or groups over others.
- **Interface and Interaction Bias**: The design of the user interface can also be a source of bias. The way options are presented, the defaults that are chosen, or the types of inputs the interface encourages can steer users toward biased outcomes [21].

These biases manifest in harmful ways. Text-to-image models prompted with "a doctor" or "a CEO" may disproportionately generate images of white men, reinforcing occupational stereotypes [37]. Models trained on biased health data may lead to unfair clinical decisions and exacerbate existing health disparities [38]. The challenge is compounded by the fact that fairness itself is not a single, easily defined concept; what constitutes a "fair" outcome can be highly context-dependent and subject to debate [39].

4.6.2 Methodologies for Bias Detection

Before bias can be mitigated, it must first be detected, and a range of methodologies has been developed for auditing and quantifying bias in GAI systems, as outlined in a comprehensive review. One common approach is adversarial testing, which involves deliberately probing the model to reveal hidden biases. This can include counterfactual fairness testing, where a sensitive attribute—such as changing a name from "Emily" to "Lakisha"—is altered while all other inputs remain constant to observe how the output changes. Stress testing, another facet of this method, subjects the model to extreme or unusual inputs to assess its performance under pressure. Statistical analysis offers another robust avenue for bias detection by using statistical tools to compare outputs across different demographic groups. Chi-square tests can identify significant differences in the distribution of categorical outcomes, such as the allocation of job roles to different genders, while T-tests and ANOVA can be used to compare continuous outcomes, such as sentiment scores generated for different racial groups. To make bias auditing more efficient and accessible, automated auditing tools like IBM's AI Fairness 360 (AIF360) and Microsoft's Fairlearn provide comprehensive sets of fairness metrics and bias mitigation algorithms, enabling developers to integrate bias detection directly into their workflows. Additionally, open-set bias detection offers a more exploratory approach, aiming to uncover unforeseen biases without relying on predefined categories. This often involves using large language models to dynamically construct a knowledge base of potential societal biases, thereby enabling the detection of subtler, previously unconsidered forms of bias.

Once bias has been identified, the next step is to implement targeted mitigation strategies that address its root causes without compromising the model's performance or utility. These strategies may involve pre-processing techniques, such as rebalancing or augmenting training datasets to ensure fair representation across demographic groups, or in-processing methods, where fairness constraints and regularization terms are incorporated directly into the model's learning process. Post-processing approaches can also be applied, adjusting the model's outputs to meet fairness criteria without retraining the underlying system. In the context of GAI, bias mitigation must be approached as a continuous process, with regular re-evaluation to account for model updates, domain shifts, and evolving societal norms. By integrating bias detection and mitigation into the broader GenAIOps lifecycle, organizations can ensure that fairness is not treated as an afterthought but as a core design and operational principle.

4.6.3 A Multi-pronged Approach to Bias Mitigation

There is no single "magic bullet" for fixing bias. Effective mitigation requires a layered strategy that addresses the problem at multiple stages of the GAI lifecycle. This approach can be categorized into three main types of intervention [21]:

- **Pre-processing (Data-Centric Mitigation)**: These strategies focus on fixing the data before it is used to train the model. This is often the most effective approach as it addresses the root cause of many biases. Techniques include
  - **Diverse and Representative Data Collection**: Actively sourcing data that better reflects the diversity of the target population [37].
  - **Re-sampling**: Over-sampling data from minority groups or under-sampling data from majority groups to create a more balanced dataset.
  - **Data Augmentation and Synthetic Data Generation**: Creating new, artificial data points to bolster the representation of underrepresented groups. For example, GANs can be used to generate high-quality synthetic health data for minority patient populations to improve model fairness in downstream predictive tasks [38].
- **In-Processing (Algorithm-Centric Mitigation)**: These strategies modify the model's training process to actively discourage biased decision-making. Techniques include
  - **Fairness Constraints and Regularization**: Adding terms to the model's loss function that penalize it for making disparate predictions across different groups. This forces the model to find a solution that balances accuracy with fairness [37].
  - **Adversarial Debiasing**: Training a second, "adversarial" model that tries to predict a sensitive attribute from the main model's outputs. The main model is then trained to "fool" the adversary, effectively learning to make predictions that are independent of the sensitive attribute [37].
- **Post-processing (Output-Centric Mitigation)**: These strategies take the model's output as-is and adjust it to satisfy fairness constraints. For example, the output probabilities of a classifier can be recalibrated to ensure that error rates (e.g., false positives and false negatives) are equal across different demographic groups, a technique known as equalized odds or calibrated equalized odds post-processing [37].

The choice of mitigation strategy involves navigating a complex set of trade-offs. There is often a fundamental tension between fairness, model accuracy, and implementation complexity. For example, some debiasing techniques that improve a particular fairness metric may do so at the cost of degrading the model's overall predictive performance [21]. Furthermore, more sophisticated in-processing methods like adversarial debiasing or hypernetwork-based regularization [40] can add significant computational and engineering overhead to the development lifecycle, clashing with the need for agile deployment. This "Fairness-Accuracy-Complexity" trilemma means that there is no universally optimal solution. The selection of a mitigation strategy is a highly context-dependent decision that requires a Value-Sensitive Design approach, involving careful deliberation about which values and trade-offs are most important for a given application.

4.6.4 An Operational Framework for Responsible GAI

To make these concepts more tangible for developers and organizations, the various risks and mitigation strategies can be mapped into an operational framework. This provides a practical link between high-level ethical principles and concrete technical or procedural interventions, serving as a risk-management checklist (Table 4.4).

Table 4.4 Mapping ethical risks to mitigation strategies

Ethical risk	Description	Example	Primary mitigation strategy (category)	Specific method/ tool
Stereotype reinforcement	GenAI outputs reproduce and amplify harmful societal stereotypes about demographic groups	A text-to-image model generates "nurse" as female and "engineer" as male	Pre-processing and in-processing	Diverse data sourcing; adversarial debiasing
Disproportionate error rates	A GAI system is significantly less accurate for one demographic group than for another	A medical diagnostic GAI has a higher false negative rate for Black patients	Pre-processing and post-processing	Synthetic data generation for minority groups [38]; equalized odds post-processing [37]
Information hazards (data leakage)	The model inadvertently reveals sensitive or private information from its training data	An LLM generates text containing a real person's private contact information	Privacy-preserving technologies	Differential privacy (DP); federated learning (FL) [15]
Opaque decision-making	Users cannot understand why the GAI made a particular decision, eroding trust and accountability	A loan applicant is denied by an AI system with no reason given	Comprehension properties and XAI	Use of explainability methods like LIME/SHAP; translating XAI output with LLMs [41]
De-skilling/job displacement	GAI automates tasks in a way that diminishes human skills or replaces human workers entirely	A generative design tool automates all conceptual work, leaving architects only with final selection tasks	Purpose and interaction design	Focus on augmentation over pure automation; design for co-creation and human control [6]

4.7 Opening the Black Box: Transparency and Explainability (XAI)

Alongside fairness, transparency is a cornerstone of trustworthy AI. If users and stakeholders cannot understand how a GAI system arrives at its conclusions, it becomes impossible to verify its correctness, debug its failures, contest its decisions, or hold it accountable. The "black box" nature of many complex models like deep neural networks is a primary barrier to their adoption in high-stakes domains [6]. Explainable AI (XAI) is the field dedicated to developing methods and models that make the decision-making processes of GAI systems more understandable to humans.

4.7.1 The Transparency Imperative

The demand for transparency is not merely a technical preference; it is a fundamental requirement for human-centricity. Research shows that a lack of transparency is a key concern for users and a significant impediment to their ability to interact effectively with GAI systems [22]. Conversely, improving transparency is a direct path to building user trust [11]. In the HCAI framework, transparency and its related concepts of explainability and intelligibility are core properties that enable effective human oversight and control [6]. Without them, the user is reduced to a passive consumer of AI outputs, unable to engage in meaningful collaboration or exercise responsible judgment.

4.7.2 Methods of Explainable GAI (XGAI)

Since many of the most powerful generative and predictive models are inherently complex, much of the work in XGAI has focused on post-hoc explanation methods. These techniques do not change the underlying model but are applied after a prediction has been made to provide an interpretation of that specific decision. Two of the most prominent local explanation methods are [15] LIME (Local Interpretable Model-agnostic Explanations) and SHAP (SHapley Additive exPlanations). LIME operates by creating a simple, interpretable model—such as a linear regression—that approximates the behavior of the more complex "black box" model in the local vicinity of a single prediction. This method effectively answers the question: "Which input features were most important for this specific decision?" SHAP, on the other hand, is grounded in cooperative game theory and provides a unified measure of feature importance. For any given prediction, SHAP assigns each feature an attribution value that quantifies its contribution to shifting the model's output away from a baseline prediction, offering a more theoretically robust and consistent explanation of feature importance. These methods are powerful tools for developers and domain experts to debug models, validate their behavior, and gain insights into their decision-making logic.

However, while LIME and SHAP offer valuable interpretability, they are not without limitations. Both methods can be computationally intensive, especially for large-scale models, and their explanations may vary depending on parameter choices or the randomness inherent in the approximation process. Additionally, because they operate post-hoc, there is always a risk that the explanations they produce do not fully reflect the true internal reasoning of the model, but rather an approximation that is locally consistent. This has led researchers to explore complementary approaches, such as inherently interpretable model architectures and hybrid explanation techniques, which aim to balance predictive power with transparency from the outset. In the context of XGAI, combining post-hoc tools like LIME and SHAP with proactive design choices can create more reliable, trustworthy, and actionable insights for both developers and end-users.

4.7.3 From Technical Explanations to Human-Readable Insights

A significant challenge with methods like LIME and SHAP is that their raw output-typically a list of features and their attribution scores-can still be complex and difficult for non-expert personnel to interpret quickly and act upon [41]. This creates a "last mile" problem for explainability. A powerful emerging trend to solve this problem is the recursive use of GAI to explain GAI.

This innovative approach uses one type of GAI, typically a Large Language Model (LLM), to interpret and translate the technical output of an XGAI tool into a human-readable natural language narrative [41]. For example, in a network security context, an LSTM model might detect a DDoS attack. A post-hoc XGAI method like SHAP would then identify the key performance indicators (e.g., "uplink throughput," "packet loss rate") that contributed most to this classification. Finally, this list of technical features and scores is passed to an LLM, which generates a clear, concise explanation, such as: "An anomaly was detected because of an unusually high uplink throughput combined with a sudden spike in packet loss, which is indicative of a potential DDoS attack. Consider investigating traffic from the following sources" [41].

This meta-level application of GAI has profound implications. It suggests that achieving full transparency may not require making the primary models simpler, but rather building more sophisticated "explainer" models on top of them. This reduces the cognitive burden on human operators, accelerates incident response, and bridges the gap between opaque detection and actionable mitigation [42]. However, it also introduces a new layer of abstraction and a new potential point of failure. How can we ensure the LLM's narrative explanation is a faithful and accurate representation of the underlying XAI analysis? This opens up a new and critical research area in "Explainable Explainability" and shifts the human's role in the loop. Instead of interpreting raw technical data, the human becomes a supervisor of a GAI-generated explanation, tasked with validating the narrative itself. This creates a new "human-on-the-loop" paradigm, where the focus is on overseeing the interaction between different GAI systems.

4.8 Synthesis and Future Trajectories

The design and development of human-centric generative AI is not a monolithic practice but a dynamic and context-dependent field. The principles and methodologies discussed in this report are not applied uniformly; their implementation and prioritization vary significantly across different domains of application. This final part of the report synthesizes the preceding analysis through a series of cross-domain case studies, illustrating how these methodologies are put into practice. It culminates in a proposed integrated framework for the human-centric development lifecycle and a forward-looking agenda that identifies the most pressing unresolved challenges and promising directions for future research.

4.8.1 Methodologies in Practice: Cross-domain Case Studies

By examining how generative AI is being applied in diverse fields—from the expressive arts to critical infrastructure—we can see how the specific demands of each domain shape the approach to human-centric design.

4.8.2 The Creative Industries

In fields like visual arts, music composition, and design, generative AI is primarily used as a tool for augmentation and exploration [2]. Case studies reveal GAI's growing influence, from generating artworks that win competitions and sell at major auction houses to producing commercial music and complex 3D architectural designs [2]. Platforms like Autodesk's Dreamcatcher use generative design to rapidly produce a wide array of design alternatives based on specified constraints, freeing architects and engineers to focus on more conceptual tasks [2]. In music, GAI tools like Amper Music and AIVA assist musicians by generating melodies and harmonies, enabling them to explore novel compositions [2]. The dominant design philosophy in this domain is a form of Human-in-the-Loop, where the human acts as a director, curator, and creative partner to the GAI. The emphasis in interaction design is on providing users with fine-grained control over the generative process and tools for exploring and refining the multiple outputs produced by the GAI [24]. While this domain celebrates the acceleration of production and the democratization of creative tools, it also grapples with fundamental questions of authorship, originality, and the challenge of imbuing AI-generated content with human emotion and intentionality [2].

4.8.3 Healthcare and Medical Science

In contrast to the creative arts, the application of generative AI in healthcare and medical science is governed by the paramount values of safety, privacy, accuracy, and fairness [4]. Here, GAI is used for tasks such as generating synthetic patient data to train other models without compromising privacy, assisting in health communication by drafting empathetic responses to patient questions, and creating complex medical imagery like CT scans from text prompts [4]. The development of these systems is heavily reliant on Value-Sensitive Design to proactively embed ethical principles and on rigorous Human-in-the-Loop processes for clinical validation and oversight. For instance, any AI-drafted response to a patient must be reviewed and approved by a certified physician [4]. A human-centered approach is critical, as developing domain-specific models without involving stakeholders' risks creating tools that are not useful or are even harmful [9]. Consequently, bias mitigation is a central concern, as models trained on unrepresentative health data can perpetuate and worsen health disparities for marginalized populations [21].

4.8.4 Education and Learning

The goal of GAI in education is to create more dynamic, engaging, and inclusive learning environments through augmentation and empowerment [43]. Case studies include the use of generative AI to create complex educational assessments at scale, with human review ensuring quality [20], and the development of personalized learning chatbots like UT Sage, which acts as a tutor for students and an instructional design coach for faculty [44]. The key methodologies in this domain are participatory design and co-design, which involve students, educators, and other stakeholders directly in the design process to ensure the tools meet their pedagogical needs [45]. Interaction design focuses on striking a careful balance between automation and learner agency, creating systems that provide personalized support without undermining the student's own learning process and critical thinking skills [43].

4.8.5 High-Stakes Infrastructure (Networking and Supply Chain)

In domains responsible for critical infrastructure, such as telecommunications and supply chain management, the primary values are reliability, robustness, and efficiency. Generative AI is being explored for tasks like network monitoring and management, where it can automate the translation of user objectives into network policies and anticipate traffic patterns to prevent issues [1]. In supply chain risk management, it is used for forecasting, scenario planning, and identifying potential disruptions from unstructured data sources [5]. The dominant methodologies are a robust Human-in-the-Loop model, where human experts supervise and verify the decisions of automated systems, and a mature GenAIOps framework to ensure the scalable, resilient, and secure deployment of these critical systems [1]. The goal is to leverage AI's predictive and generative capabilities to create self-optimizing and self-healing networks that reduce manual complexity and enhance responsiveness [1].

However, realizing this vision requires careful alignment of technological innovation with stringent operational and regulatory standards. In these high-stakes environments, even minor errors can have cascading consequences, making rigorous testing, continuous monitoring, and fail-safe mechanisms indispensable. By combining the adaptability of GAI with well-defined governance protocols, organizations can ensure that these systems not only deliver enhanced performance but also uphold the trust, stability, and safety essential to critical infrastructure operations.

4.9 The Path Forward: An Integrated Framework and Research Agenda

The continued development and deployment of generative AI will require a more unified and systematic approach to human-centric design. By synthesizing the principles, methodologies, and practical lessons discussed throughout this report, it is possible to outline an integrated development lifecycle and identify the most critical areas for future research.

4.9.1 An Integrated Human-Centric Development Lifecycle

A truly mature approach to human-centric generative AI must weave together the disparate threads of design philosophy, development practice, and ethical oversight into a single, cohesive process. This report proposes an integrated lifecycle model that proceeds as follows:

1. **Phase 1: Participatory Value-Sensitive Design (PVSD).** The lifecycle begins not with code, but with conversation. This phase combines the collaborative

spirit of Participatory Design with the principled framework of VSD. It involves conducting co-design workshops with all relevant stakeholders (users, domain experts, community representatives) to collaboratively define the system's purpose, identify context-specific values, and anticipate potential value tensions and ethical risks. The output of this phase is a set of clear, value-grounded design requirements.

2. **Phase 2**: Agile Development with HITL and XGAI by Design. The value-based requirements from Phase 1 inform the Agile development process. Sprints are focused on building a system where Human-in-the-Loop mechanisms are not an afterthought but are designed in from the start to provide necessary oversight and control. Similarly, Explainable GAI (XGAI) capabilities are treated as a core feature, ensuring that the system is transparent and interpretable by design.
3. **Phase 3: Governance via GenAIOps**. The entire development and deployment process is supported and governed by a mature GenAIOps pipeline. This framework automates the testing, deployment, and monitoring of the entire GAI application stack, including models, prompts, and RAG systems. It enforces the governance rules established in Phase 1, ensuring reliability, security, and reproducibility.
4. **Phase 4: Continuous Multidimensional Evaluation**. Running parallel to all other phases is a continuous loop of multidimensional evaluation. At every stage—from initial prototype to deployed system—the GAI is assessed against a holistic set of metrics covering output quality, user experience, and ethical integrity. Feedback from these evaluations, including real-world user feedback, is fed back into the PVSD and Agile processes, enabling iterative refinement and ensuring the system remains aligned with human values over its entire lifecycle. The figure illustrates the integrated human-centric development lifecycle, showing how participatory value-sensitive design, agile development with HITL and XGAI, GenAIOps governance, and continuous multidimensional evaluation are interconnected in an iterative, feedback-driven process. Figure 4.2 presents the human-centric development lifecycle, outlining four iterative stages—participatory value-sensitive design, agile development with HITL and explainable AI, governance through GenAIOps, and ongoing multidimensional evaluation—that work together in a continuous feedback loop.

4.9.2 Unresolved Challenges and Future Research Directions

Despite rapid progress, the field of human-centric generative GAI is still nascent, with many critical questions remaining unanswered. A forward-looking research agenda should prioritize the following areas [1]:

- **Longitudinal and Ecological Studies**: Much of the current research is based on short-term lab studies or initial deployments. There is a critical need for longitudinal research that examines the long-term impacts of sustained human-GAI collaboration on human skills, creativity, cognitive load, and overall well-being.

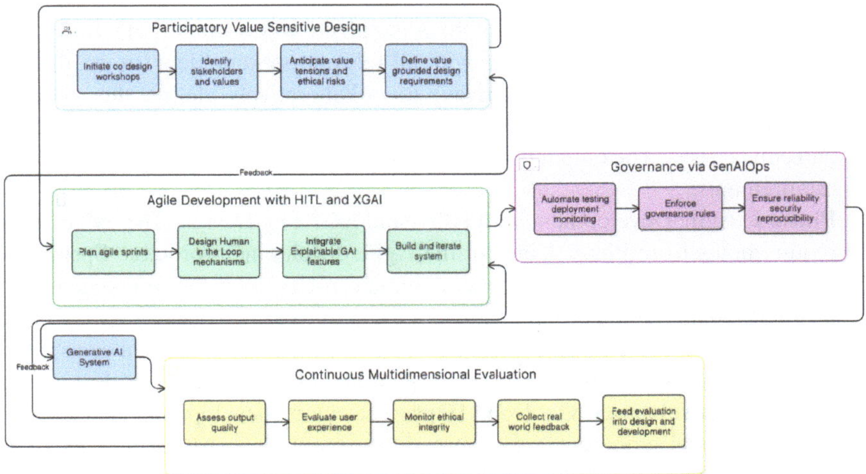

Fig. 4.2 Integrated human-centric development lifecycle

- **The Governance of Hybrid Systems**: As agency becomes increasingly distributed between humans and GAI agents, new legal, ethical, and organizational frameworks are needed to manage accountability. Research is required to develop robust models for assigning responsibility in complex socio-technical systems where causal chains are often opaque.
- **The "More-Than-Human" Turn**: The current focus of HCGAI is, by definition, on human needs and values. However, some researchers argue that this anthropocentric view may be insufficient for addressing the broader impacts of GAI [6]. Future research should critically examine this perspective, exploring design approaches that consider the technology's impact on ecological systems, non-human entities, and planetary health.
- **Scaling Deliberative and Participatory Processes**: The deep, qualitative, and often time-consuming methods of participatory design and VSD are in tension with the culture of rapid, large-scale deployment that characterizes the modern technology industry. A major research challenge is to develop new methods and tools that can scale these deliberative processes, allowing the rich insights from stakeholder engagement to effectively guide development at the speed and scale required by the real world.
- **Defining and Measuring Fairness**: While many techniques exist for bias mitigation, the fundamental concepts of fairness remain contested and context-dependent. Further interdisciplinary research is needed to develop more nuanced definitions of fairness and more reliable frameworks for measuring it, moving beyond purely technical metrics to incorporate stakeholder perceptions and societal values [46].

By addressing these challenges, the research community can help guide the evolution of generative AI away from being a purely technological force and toward its potential as a true partner in enhancing human creativity, augmenting human intelligence, and fostering a more equitable and prosperous society.

References

1. Mapping the Landscape of Generative AI in Network Monitoring and Management—arXiv. Retrieved August 3, 2025, from https://arxiv.org/html/2502.08576v2
2. (PDF) The Architecture of Generative AI and Its Role in the Creative.... Retrieved August 3, 2025, from https://www.researchgate.net/publication/393398625_The_Architecture_of_Generative_AI_and_Its_Role_in_the_Creative_Industry
3. An HCI-Centric Survey and Taxonomy of Human-Generative-AI.... Retrieved August 3, 2025, from https://engineering.purdue.edu/cdesign/wp/wp-content/uploads/2023/10/hgaisurvey.pdf
4. Leveraging Generative AI and Large Language Models: A Comprehensive Roadmap for Healthcare Integration—PMC. Retrieved August 3, 2025, from https://pmc.ncbi.nlm.nih.gov/articles/PMC10606429/
5. A Comprehensive Framework for Selecting the Best Human-Centric Generative AI Model for Supply Chain Risk Management—viXra.org. Retrieved August 3, 2025, from https://vixra.org/pdf/2409.0161v1.pdf
6. Understanding Human-Centred AI: A Review of Its Defining Elements.... Retrieved August 3, 2025, from https://www.tandfonline.com/doi/full/10.1080/0144929X.2024.2448719
7. Human in the Loop?—Alexander von Humboldt Institut für Internet und Gesellschaft | HIIG. Retrieved August 3, 2025, from https://www.hiig.de/en/project/human-in-the-loop/
8. Exploring the Supportive Role of Artificial Intelligence in.... Retrieved August 3, 2025, from https://research.tilburguniversity.edu/files/103581403/Exploring_the_supportive_role.pdf
9. arxiv.org. Retrieved August 3, 2025, from https://arxiv.org/html/2507.16207v1
10. La Independiente: An AI-Enhanced Platform Co-Designed with Latin.... Retrieved August 3, 2025, from https://par.nsf.gov/servlets/purl/10490575
11. Harnessing the Power of AI in Qualitative Research: Exploring, Using and Redesigning ChatGPT—ResearchGate. Retrieved August 3, 2025, from https://www.researchgate.net/publication/390100640_Harnessing_the_Power_of_AI_in_Qualitative_Research_Exploring_Using_and_Redesigning_ChatGPT
12. (PDF) Human-Centered NLP Fact-Checking: Co-designing with Fact.... Retrieved August 3, 2025, from https://www.researchgate.net/publication/373116399_Human-centered_NLP_Fact-checking_Co-Designing_with_Fact-checkers_using_Matchmaking_for_AI
13. A Value Sensitive Design Perspective on AI Biases—ScholarSpace. Retrieved August 3, 2025, from https://scholarspace.manoa.hawaii.edu/bitstreams/955625fc-e895-416b-81cd-ab0a5d4a0d7c/download
14. Mapping Value Sensitive Design onto AI for Social Good Principles. Retrieved August 3, 2025, from https://pubmed.ncbi.nlm.nih.gov/34790942/
15. (PDF) Ethical Imperatives in AI Design: A Comprehensive.... Retrieved August 3, 2025, from https://www.researchgate.net/publication/393275119_Ethical_Imperatives_in_AI_Design_A_Comprehensive_Framework_for_Risk_Mitigation_and_Responsible_Innovation
16. Value-Sensitive Algorithm Design: Method, Case Study, and Lessons—ResearchGate. Retrieved August 3, 2025, from https://www.researchgate.net/publication/328691430_Value-Sensitive_Algorithm_Design_Method_Case_Study_and_Lessons
17. What is Human-in-the-Loop (HITL) in AI & ML—Google Cloud. Retrieved August 3, 2025, from https://cloud.google.com/discover/human-in-the-loop
18. Humans in the Loop: The Design of Interactive AI Systems | Stanford HAI. Retrieved August 3, 2025, from https://hai.stanford.edu/news/humans-loop-design-interactive-ai-systems

19. Human-in-the-Loop Automation Lifecycle—UiPath. Retrieved August 3, 2025, from https://www.uipath.com/platform/agentic-automation/human-in-the-loop
20. An Illustration of the Grounds, Claims, and Inferences in the Interpretive Argument—ResearchGate. Retrieved August 3, 2025, from https://www.researchgate.net/figure/An-illustration-of-the-grounds-claims-and-inferences-in-the-interpretive-argument_fig7_363382233
21. Addressing 6 Challenges in Generative AI for Digital Health: A Scoping Review—PMC. Retrieved August 3, 2025, from https://pmc.ncbi.nlm.nih.gov/articles/PMC11115971/
22. Redefining Qualitative Analysis in the AI Era: Utilizing ChatGPT for Efficient Thematic Analysis—arXiv. Retrieved August 3, 2025, from https://arxiv.org/html/2309.10771v3
23. Prompting Generative AI with Interaction-Augmented Instructions—arXiv. Retrieved August 3, 2025, from https://arxiv.org/html/2503.02874v1
24. Toward General Design Principles for Generative AI...—arXiv. Retrieved August 3, 2025, from https://arxiv.org/pdf/2301.05578
25. Accelerating Software Development Agile Teams with Generative AI | Milestone. Retrieved August 3, 2025, from https://mstone.ai/blog/accelerating-software-development-agile-teams-with-generative-ai/
26. How an AI-Enabled Software Product Development Life Cycle Will Fuel Innovation—McKinsey. Retrieved August 3, 2025, from https://www.mckinsey.com/industries/technology-media-and-telecommunications/our-insights/how-an-ai-enabled-software-product-development-life-cycle-will-fuel-innovation
27. The AI Productivity Paradox in Software Engineering: Balancing Efficiency and Human Skill Retention—SD Times. Retrieved August 3, 2025, from https://sdtimes.com/agile/the-ai-productivity-paradox-in-software-engineering-balancing-efficiency-and-human-skill-retention/
28. Agile in the Age of AI: A Practitioner's Guide to Evolving Scrum | by Yuji Isobe—Medium. Retrieved August 3, 2025, from https://medium.com/@yujiisobe/agile-in-the-age-of-ai-a-practitioners-guide-to-evolving-scrum-a94966326571
29. Transforming AI Excellence: Empowering with MLOps Mastery—Intellias. Retrieved August 3, 2025, from https://intellias.com/empowering-ai-with-mlops/
30. What is MLOps?—Machine Learning Operations Explained—AWS. Retrieved August 3, 2025, from https://aws.amazon.com/what-is/mlops/
31. What Is MLOps?—IBM. Retrieved August 3, 2025, from https://www.ibm.com/think/topics/mlops
32. NVIDIA MLOps Ecosystem—Machine Learning Operations. Retrieved August 3, 2025, from https://www.nvidia.com/en-us/data-center/solutions/mlops/
33. Generative AI Operations for Organizations with MLOps Investments.... Retrieved August 3, 2025, from https://learn.microsoft.com/en-us/azure/architecture/ai-ml/guide/genaiops-for-mlops
34. Understanding Human Evaluation Metrics in AI: What They Are and How They Work. Retrieved August 3, 2025, from https://galileo.ai/blog/human-evaluation-metrics-ai
35. Bias in Artificial Intelligence for Medical Imaging: Fundamentals, Detection, Avoidance, Mitigation, Challenges, Ethics, and Prospects—Diagnostic and Interventional Radiology. Retrieved August 3, 2025, from https://dirjournal.org/articles/bias-in-artificial-intelligence-for-medical-imaging-fundamentals-detection-avoidance-mitigation-challenges-ethics-and-prospects/dir.2024.242854
36. A Taxonomy of the Biases of the Images Created by Generative Artificial Intelligence—arXiv. Retrieved August 3, 2025, from https://arxiv.org/html/2407.01556v1
37. (PDF) Ethical AI Development: Mitigating Bias in Generative Models. Retrieved August 3, 2025, from https://www.researchgate.net/publication/382489481_Ethical_AI_Development_Mitigating_Bias_in_Generative_Models
38. Generative AI Mitigates Representation Bias and Improves Model Fairness Through Synthetic Health Data—PMC. Retrieved August 3, 2025, from https://pmc.ncbi.nlm.nih.gov/articles/PMC12112403/
39. Fairness As An Afterthought: An American Perspective on Fairness in Model Developer-Clinician User Collaborations—PubMed Central. Retrieved August 3, 2025, from https://pmc.ncbi.nlm.nih.gov/articles/PMC10659157/

40. Improving Fairness and Mitigating MADness in Generative Models—OpenReview. Retrieved August 3, 2025, from https://openreview.net/forum?id=tL8dpJmECp
41. Interpretable Anomaly-Based DDoS Detection in AI-RAN with XAI and LLMs—ResearchGate. Retrieved August 3, 2025, from https://www.researchgate.net/publication/394100631_Interpretable_Anomaly-Based_DDoS_Detection_in_AI-RAN_with_XAI_and_LLMs
42. Interpretable Anomaly-Based DDoS Detection in AI-RAN with XAI and LLMs—arXiv. Retrieved August 3, 2025, from https://arxiv.org/pdf/2507.21193
43. Human-Centered AI for Learning—Design for Experiences—WordPress.com. Retrieved August 3, 2025, from https://exde.wordpress.com/2024/11/03/human-centered-ai-for-learning/
44. Building Responsible AI Chatbot Platforms in Higher Education: An Evidence-Based Framework from Design to Implementation—Frontiers. Retrieved August 3, 2025, from https://www.frontiersin.org/journals/education/articles/10.3389/feduc.2025.1604934/full
45. [2506.15525] "How Can We Learn and use AI at the Same Time?": Participatory Design of GenAI with High School Students—arXiv. Retrieved August 3, 2025, from https://arxiv.org/abs/2506.15525
46. On Measuring Fairness in Generative Models. Retrieved August 3, 2025, from https://proceedings.neurips.cc/paper_files/paper/2023/file/220165f9c7f51163b73c8c7fff578b4e-Paper-Conference.pdf
47. NLP for Maternal Healthcare: Perspectives and Guiding Principles in the Age of LLMs—ACM FAccT. Retrieved August 3, 2025, from https://facctconference.org/static/papers24/facct24-97.pdf
48. MLOps so AI Can Scale—McKinsey. Retrieved August 3, 2025, from https://www.mckinsey.com/capabilities/mckinsey-digital/our-insights/mlops-so-ai-can-scale
49. Human-Centered Evaluation of Explainable AI Applications: A Systematic Review—Frontiers. Retrieved August 3, 2025, from https://www.frontiersin.org/journals/artificial-intelligence/articles/10.3389/frai.2024.1456486/full
50. Foundation Metrics for Evaluating Effectiveness of Healthcare Conversations Powered by Generative AI—PMC. Retrieved August 3, 2025, from https://pmc.ncbi.nlm.nih.gov/articles/PMC10980701/
51. Evaluating Human-AI Collaboration: A Review and Methodological Framework—arXiv. Retrieved August 3, 2025, from https://arxiv.org/html/2407.19098v2
52. A Quantum Probability Approach to Improving Human–AI Decision Making—PMC. Retrieved August 3, 2025, from https://pmc.ncbi.nlm.nih.gov/articles/PMC11854726/
53. Revisiting Technical Bias Mitigation Strategies Abdoul Jalil Djiberou Mahamadou, Artem A. Trotsyuk Center for Biomedical Ethics—arXiv. Retrieved August 3, 2025, from https://arxiv.org/pdf/2410.17433
54. Objectives and Obstacles of Artificial Intelligence in Education | Request PDF. Retrieved August 3, 2025, from https://www.researchgate.net/publication/379424311_Objectives_and_Obstacles_of_Artificial_Intelligence_in_Education
55. A Generative AI-Driven Interactive Listening Assessment Task—PMC. Retrieved August 3, 2025, from https://pmc.ncbi.nlm.nih.gov/articles/PMC11571064/
56. The Promise of Micro-credentials and Learning and Employment Record Technologies for Youth and K-12 Schools—ERIC. Retrieved August 3, 2025, from https://files.eric.ed.gov/fulltext/ED671225.pdf

Chapter 5
Implementing Generative AI in Practice

The chapter Implementing Human-Centric Generative AI in Practice focuses on the practical steps and strategies for integrating human-centered principles into the development and deployment of generative AI systems. It outlines how organizations can apply ethical guidelines, user-centered design, and fairness considerations at every stage, from data collection to model training and evaluation. The chapter provides insights into real-world applications, showcasing how generative AI can be used in diverse fields like healthcare, education, and content creation while ensuring that systems are transparent, accountable, and inclusive. It discusses the importance of user feedback loops, ongoing testing, and iteration to ensure that AI tools remain aligned with human needs and values. Additionally, the chapter covers the challenges of scaling human-centric AI solutions and the need for collaboration among stakeholders—including technologists, policymakers, and affected communities—to create robust governance frameworks and regulatory standards. Overall, it emphasizes that the successful implementation of generative AI requires a balanced approach that considers both technical excellence and social responsibility.

5.1 Foundations of Human-Centric Generative AI

The advent of generative artificial intelligence (GAI) marks a significant technological inflection point, with capabilities to create content—text, images, code, and more—that is often indistinguishable from human output [1]. While the potential for GAI to transform industries and augment productivity is immense, its rapid proliferation has also surfaced profound questions regarding its alignment with human values, its impact on society, and the ethical guardrails necessary for its responsible deployment [2]. This has catalyzed a paradigm shift away from purely performance-driven AI development toward a more holistic, human-centric approach. This report provides a comprehensive framework for implementing human-centric generative AI

T. Hazra et al., *Building Human-Centered Generative AI*,
https://doi.org/10.1007/978-3-032-21412-6_5

(HCG-AI), moving from foundational principles to practical, sector-specific applications. It outlines a structured lifecycle for HCG-AI, examines the multifaceted challenges inherent in its implementation, and provides actionable guidelines for developers, organizational leaders, and policymakers. By grounding theoretical concepts in real-world scenarios, this analysis aims to provide a blueprint for architecting GAI systems that not only perform tasks but also augment human intelligence, enhance well-being, and contribute to a more equitable and sustainable future.

5.1.1 Redefining Intelligence: From Automation to Augmentation

The discourse surrounding artificial intelligence has historically been dominated by a focus on automation—the replacement of human tasks with machine processes to achieve greater efficiency and speed [3]. However, the limitations and unintended consequences of this technology-first approach have become increasingly apparent, leading to the rise of a new philosophy: Human-centered AI (HCAI). This paradigm reframes the objective of AI development from replacement to empowerment, establishing a new set of principles that prioritize human needs and values at the core of system design and operation.

Defining the Human-Centered AI (HCAI) Paradigm

Human-centered AI (HCAI) is an approach to the design, development, and deployment of artificial intelligence systems that prioritizes human needs, values, and capabilities [4]. Its fundamental goal is to create AI that amplifies and augments human abilities rather than displacing them [5]. This philosophy posits that the most effective systems emerge from a symbiotic relationship where "human + AI" is superior to either acting in isolation [5]. HCAI seeks to preserve meaningful human control, ensuring that AI systems meet human needs while operating transparently, delivering equitable outcomes, and respecting fundamental rights such as privacy [5].

This paradigm inherently recognizes that AI systems are not merely technical artifacts but are socio-technical systems that interact with and impact users, stakeholders, and society at large [6]. Consequently, HCAI is an interdisciplinary endeavor, necessitating close collaboration among computer scientists, developers, designers, ethicists, psychologists, sociologists, and domain experts [4]. This collaborative process is essential for creating AI that is not only technically robust but also transparent, explainable, and accountable, thereby addressing the complex ethical, social, and cultural implications of its deployment [4].

Core Principles: Empathy, Ethics, and Empowerment

The HCAI paradigm is built upon a set of foundational principles that guide every stage of the AI lifecycle. These principles are not treated as optional features or post-development checks; rather, they are integrated into the design process from its inception [3]. The key principles include empathy and understanding the user, where HCAI begins with a deep understanding of user needs, preferences, behaviors, and pain points. This involves engaging directly with users and stakeholders to ensure the AI solution is intuitive, beneficial, and finely tuned to real-world contexts [4]. Ethical considerations and bias mitigation form another pillar, emphasizing that ethics are a core component, not an add-on. HCAI mandates the proactive identification and mitigation of potential biases in data and algorithms to ensure fairness, prevent discriminatory outcomes, and respect user privacy and data security [3]. User involvement in the design process is also central, as HCAI advocates for participatory design methodologies where users are active collaborators throughout development. This co-creation helps identify and mitigate biases, leading to more effective and equitable solutions [4].

Accessibility and inclusivity are equally important, requiring AI systems to be designed for all users, including those with disabilities. Development teams should embrace diverse user groups to ensure inclusivity and prevent the digital divide from widening [4]. Transparency and explainability are critical, ensuring that users understand how and why an AI system makes its decisions. Such explainability builds trust, ensures accountability, and enables users to make informed judgments about the AI's outputs [3].

Continuous feedback and improvement are necessary, as HCAI systems are not static; they require mechanisms for ongoing user feedback, which are then used for iterative improvements to remain aligned with evolving human needs and values over time [4]. Finally, a balance between automation and human control is maintained. A central tenet of HCAI is to augment, not replace, human skills, striking a careful balance that automates routine or burdensome tasks while preserving human agency, judgment, and control, especially in high-stakes decisions [4].

Contrasting HCAI with Traditional AI Development Philosophies

The distinction between HCAI and traditional AI development is not merely methodological but philosophical. It represents a fundamental re-evaluation of the purpose and measure of success for an AI system. Traditional AI development has often been technology-centric, prioritizing the optimization of technical performance metrics such as accuracy, speed, and return on investment (ROI) [3]. In this model, the human user is frequently positioned as a passive recipient or observer of the AI's output.

HCAI, in contrast, adopts a human-first orientation. Its primary focus is on usability, trust, and alignment with human values, positioning the user as an active

Table 5.1 A comparative analysis of traditional AI and human-centered AI paradigms (Adapted from Tredence, 2025 [3])

Aspect	Traditional AI	Human-centered AI (HCAI)
Primary focus	Accuracy, speed, and automation	Usability, trust, and human values
User role	End-user or passive observer	Active collaborator and partner
Decision-making	Often opaque or a "black box"	Transparent and explainable
Feedback loops	Rare or conducted only post-deployment	Continuous, iterative, and user-driven
Ethics and fairness	Considered optionally or as a compliance check	Integrated by design from the initial phase
User experience (UX)	Not always prioritized	A core, foundational component
Oversight	Primarily machine-dominated	Emphasizes "human-in-the-loop" or human oversight
Purpose of deployment	Maximize output, efficiency, or ROI	Solve human-centric, real-world problems and enhance well-being

collaborator in a symbiotic relationship with the technology [3]. This shift necessitates a broader definition of success. While a traditional AI model might be considered successful if it achieves 99% accuracy, an HCAI system is only successful if it also earns user trust, is perceived as fair, enhances the user's capabilities, and contributes positively to their well-being. This introduces a "double bottom line" approach, where leaders must balance profitability with societal and individual empowerment [7].

This redefinition is not without its challenges. There can be inherent tension between optimizing for raw model performance and implementing human-centric features. For instance, operationalizing fairness constraints or adding layers of explainability might, in some cases, slightly reduce a model's raw predictive accuracy or increase computational overhead [3]. A traditional, performance-driven approach would view this as a net loss. An HCAI approach, however, recognizes that the resulting gains in user trust, regulatory alignment, and long-term adoption far outweigh the marginal cost in raw performance. Therefore, the successful implementation of HCAI requires a strategic commitment from organizational leadership to expand the definition of value beyond purely technical or financial key performance indicators (KPIs). It is a move from asking "how can we automate this task?" to "how can we solve this human-centric, real-world problem?" [3]. Table 5.1 provides a structured comparison of these two paradigms.

5.1.2 The Human-Centric GenAI Lifecycle

To move HCAI from a set of abstract principles to a concrete implementation strategy, a structured and actionable lifecycle is required. While traditional data science has relied on frameworks like the cross-industry standard process for data mining (CRISP-DM), the unique characteristics of generative AI—such as its reliance on large language models (LLMs), prompt engineering, and techniques like retrieval-augmented generation (RAG)—necessitate an adapted methodology [1]. This section outlines a modern GenAI lifecycle and details how human-centered principles can be systematically integrated into each phase.

A Phase-by-Phase Implementation Framework

The modern GenAI lifecycle can be conceptualized as a seven-phase process that guides a project from initial ideation to long-term operation and improvement. This framework provides a structured path for teams creating GAI-powered applications like chatbots, virtual assistants, or content generation tools [1]. The phases are as follows:

1. **Scoping (Problem Definition)**: This initial phase involves a clear definition of the business problem, project goals, and requirements [8]. It sets the foundation by identifying a high-impact, feasible application, aligning stakeholders, and determining how success will be measured. A critical part of this phase is assessing whether GAI is the appropriate tool for the problem and considering the associated risks and costs [8].
2. **Data Investigation**: Here, the team identifies and sources the data that will be used to supplement the core LLM, often through a RAG architecture [1]. RAG enables the model to access up-to-date, external information, significantly enhancing the relevance and accuracy of its responses [1]. This phase focuses on assessing data availability, quality, and relevance for the specific use case [1].
3. **Data Preparation**: This step involves cleaning, formatting, and structuring the selected data for optimal use by the GAI model. For many modern GAI applications, this includes the specialized process of embedding data into a vector store database, a step tailored to the needs of AI models that is not typically found in traditional data preparation [1].
4. **Development (Model Customization and Integration)**: In this phase, the application is built. This involves selecting an appropriate foundation model, designing effective prompts (the natural language instructions that guide the model's output), integrating the RAG system, and potentially fine-tuning the LLM on domain-specific data to improve its performance [1].
5. **Evaluation**: The developed GAI application undergoes rigorous testing. This evaluation is multifaceted, assessing not only the technical correctness and performance of the model but also the quality of its output in terms of readability, reliability, and alignment with business objectives [1].
6. **Deployment**: The finalized application is deployed into its intended production environment. This involves setting up the necessary infrastructure for hosting, scaling, and managing the application to ensure smooth integration with existing systems and workflows [1].

7. **Monitoring and Improvement**: This final, continuous phase involves monitoring the deployed application's performance, user satisfaction, and operational efficiency [1]. Based on performance data and user feedback, regular updates and improvements are made, ensuring the system evolves and remains effective over time.

Integrating Human-Centered Design Principles at Each Stage

A truly human-centric approach requires that the principles outlined in Sect. 5.1 are not just discussed but are actively operationalized at every stage of this lifecycle. This means weaving human-centric practices into the technical workflow, transforming the process from a purely engineering exercise into a collaborative, socio-technical one. Table 5.2 provides a detailed breakdown of how these principles can be integrated.

Comparative Analysis: GenAI Lifecycle Versus CRISP-DM

To better situate this modern lifecycle, it is useful to compare it with the well-established CRISP-DM framework. While both methodologies share foundational goals, the GenAI lifecycle incorporates steps and considerations specific to the development of advanced AI systems [1].

- **Problem Definition Versus Business Understanding**: These initial phases are highly similar in both frameworks, focusing on understanding the core problem and setting clear project objectives [1].
- **Data Investigation Versus Data Understanding**: Both involve assessing data sources. However, the GenAI lifecycle's *data investigation* is specifically focused on the suitability of data for RAG, a technique unique to GAI. CRISP-DM's *data understanding* is more general, covering all aspects of data relevant to a traditional data mining problem [1].
- **Data Preparation**: While both include a data preparation phase, the GenAI lifecycle introduces a specialized technical step: embedding data into vector store databases. This is a crucial process for enabling efficient information retrieval by LLMs and is a significant departure from the standard data transformation and cleaning tasks in CRISP-DM [1].
- **Development Versus Modeling**: In CRISP-DM, *modeling* typically involves selecting and training statistical or traditional machine learning models. In the GenAI lifecycle, *development* is centered on prompt engineering, model selection (often of pre-trained foundation models), and potential fine-tuning, reflecting a different set of technical skills and processes [1].
- **Evaluation**: Both frameworks include a rigorous evaluation phase. However, GAI evaluation is often more user-centric, focusing on qualitative aspects like the readability, helpfulness, and overall user experience of the generated output, whereas CRISP-DM evaluation may lean more heavily on statistical metrics like accuracy or error rates [1].

Table 5.2 Integrating human-centered principles into the GenAI lifecycle

Lifecycle phase	Key activities	Human-centric integration points
Scoping	Define business problem, goals, and success metrics	Conduct participatory problem-framing workshops with diverse stakeholders, including end-users and impacted communities [4]. Perform an initial ethical impact assessment (EIA) to identify potential harms and societal risks upfront [9]. Define success metrics that include user trust, satisfaction, and well-being, not just technical performance [10]
Data investigation	Source and assess data for relevance, quality, and suitability for RAG	Audit data sources for representation, fairness, and potential biases [3]. Involve domain experts and diverse review teams to evaluate data for cultural sensitivities and inclusivity [11]. Assess data for potential privacy infringements and ensure compliance with data protection regulations [12]
Data preparation	Clean, format, and embed data into vector stores	Implement data anonymization and privacy-preserving techniques during preparation [13]. Document data lineage and transformations to ensure transparency and traceability [9]
Development	Select model, engineer prompts, integrate RAG, fine-tune	Use co-design and participatory workshops with end-users to craft and refine prompts [4]. Build in "explainability" features that help users understand why the GAI generated a particular output [3]. Design interfaces that clearly communicate the system's capabilities and limitations [14]
Evaluation	Test for correctness, performance, and reliability	Go beyond automated metrics; employ human evaluation to assess subjective qualities like fluency, coherence, helpfulness, and human-likeness [15]. Conduct usability testing with representative users to identify UX issues [14]. Perform "red teaming" and bias audits to test for harmful or unfair outputs [16]
Deployment	Integrate the solution into the user environment	Develop clear user onboarding materials and training that set realistic expectations [3]. Be transparent with users about where and how GAI is being used, including clear disclosure when a user is interacting with an AI and not a human [13]
Monitoring and improvement	Track performance, user satisfaction, and operational efficiency	Establish robust and accessible feedback channels for users to report issues, biases, or unexpected behavior [4]. Continuously monitor user satisfaction and task success rates [15]. Use this feedback to guide an iterative cycle of model updates and prompt refinement, treating the system as an evolving entity [1]

- **Deployment**: The deployment phases are similar in their goal of integrating the solution into the user's environment. However, GAI deployment can involve more complex infrastructure to handle the computational demands of large models [1].
- **Monitoring and Improvement**: This is a key differentiator. The GenAI lifecycle formalizes a continuous *monitoring and improvement* phase, acknowledging that GAI systems are dynamic and evolve with user interaction. While CRISP-DM implies post-deployment support, it does not have an equivalent, structured phase dedicated to iterative improvement based on ongoing user feedback and performance monitoring [1].

This final point underscores a profound shift in how AI systems are conceptualized. The explicit inclusion of a continuous improvement loop, driven by user feedback, reframes the GAI application not as a static, finished product but as a dynamic, co-evolving socio-technical system. This has significant implications for governance and accountability. If the system is constantly learning and changing based on its interactions, then oversight cannot be a one-time, pre-deployment checklist. Instead, ethical reviews, bias audits, and impact assessments must become continuous, operationalized processes embedded within the organization. Accountability, therefore, shifts from the question of "who built the initial model?" to the ongoing responsibility of "who is stewarding the system's evolution?" This necessitates new organizational structures, such as dedicated AI ethics boards or governance committees, tasked with overseeing the AI's entire lifespan and navigating the value-laden decisions that arise during its continuous adaptation [9].

5.2 Navigating the Implementation Landscape: Challenges and Mitigation

The path to implementing human-centric generative AI is fraught with challenges that span the technical, organizational, and ethical domains. While the principles of HCAI provide a clear North Star, the practical journey requires navigating a complex landscape of legacy systems, entrenched cultures, technical limitations, and profound ethical questions. Acknowledging and proactively addressing these hurdles are a prerequisite for any successful HCG-AI initiative. This section provides a comprehensive analysis of these challenges and offers evidence-based strategies for their mitigation.

5.2.1 The Spectrum of Implementation Challenges

The obstacles to HCG-AI are not monolithic; they emerge from the technology itself, the organizations attempting to deploy it, and the human users who are meant to benefit from it. A holistic implementation strategy must address all three dimensions concurrently.

Technical Hurdles: Explainability, Robustness, and Security

At the core of HCG-AI implementation lie significant technical challenges that directly impact user trust and system reliability.

Many advanced GAI models, particularly those based on the transformer architecture (which underpins most LLMs), operate as "black boxes" [3]. Their internal decision-making processes are so complex that even their creators cannot fully trace why a specific input led to a particular output. This opacity is a major barrier to adoption, especially in high-stakes domains like healthcare, finance, or law, where understanding the rationale behind a decision is critical for trust, accountability, and regulatory compliance [3]. The inability to debug LLMs effectively to improve their credibility and trace the source of erroneous or biased information remains a significant research challenge [5].

For an AI to be trustworthy, it must be robust, that is, safe, reliable, and capable of functioning predictably even in uncertain or dynamic environments [17]. This includes having fault tolerance, where the system can handle unexpected inputs or partial failures gracefully without catastrophic consequences [17]. The probabilistic nature of GAI means that it can sometimes "hallucinate," generating plausible but factually incorrect information, which undermines its reliability [18]. Ensuring consistent, high-quality output is a continuous technical challenge.

GAI systems are susceptible to a range of security threats. These include traditional cyber-threats aimed at the underlying infrastructure, as well as AI-specific attacks like "prompt injection," where malicious actors craft inputs designed to bypass safety filters and trick the model into generating harmful or unintended content [17]. Protecting the system, its data, and its users from such threats is a critical and ongoing technical requirement.

Organizational Inertia: Leadership, Culture, and Workforce Transformation

Perhaps even more formidable than the technical hurdles are the organizational barriers that can stifle HCG-AI initiatives before they even begin.

- **Resistance to Change and Lack of Leadership Buy-In**: Organizational transformation is inherently difficult, and the introduction of a disruptive technology like GAI often meets with significant resistance. This can stem from psychological factors among employees, such as fear of the unknown, loss of control, or anxiety about job displacement [19]. This resistance is compounded when there is a lack of clear and committed leadership buy-in. Leaders may hesitate due to concerns about the high costs, potential disruption to existing operations, or a fundamental skepticism about the efficacy of a human-centric approach, which can be perceived as slower and more resource-intensive than traditional AI development [3]. Indeed, a lack of leadership support is a primary reason why a majority of large-scale change programs fail to achieve their goals [20].

- **Workforce Disruption and the Skills Gap**: GAI is poised to significantly impact a large percentage of the global workforce, automating or augmenting tasks across a wide range of professions [7]. This creates an urgent need for a culture of continuous learning, supported by robust reskilling and retraining programs to equip employees with the skills necessary to work alongside AI [7]. However, many organizations lack the strategic foresight or investment to manage this transition effectively, creating a gap between the skills required for an AI-enabled future and the current capabilities of the workforce [21]. This includes not only technical skills but also uniquely human-centric skills like critical thinking, ethical reasoning, and collaboration, which become more valuable as AI handles routine tasks [22].
- **Fostering Cross-Disciplinary Collaboration**: A core tenet of HCAI is the integration of diverse expertise. However, creating effective collaboration between technically minded developers, user-focused designers, abstract-thinking ethicists, and domain-specific end-users is a profound cultural challenge [3]. These groups often operate with different vocabularies, priorities, and problem-solving methodologies. Without a common lexicon and shared goals, even well-intentioned efforts can devolve into misunderstandings and stall progress. Building a truly collaborative culture is as much a part of the HCG-AI project as building the technology itself [3].

The Human Element: Cognitive Biases, Trust, and Adoption Barriers

Ultimately, the success of HCG-AI depends on its reception by human users and society at large. Several psychological and social factors can act as significant barriers to adoption.

- **The Role of Emotion in Adoption**: The decision to adopt a new technology is not purely rational; it is heavily influenced by human emotions, particularly fear [19]. Concerns about job loss, loss of autonomy, or the opaque nature of AI can evoke strong negative emotions that cannot be overcome by simply communicating objective data about the system's benefits. Acknowledging and addressing these emotional concerns through transparent communication and stakeholder involvement is crucial for building acceptance [19].
- **Building and Maintaining Trust**: Trust is the cornerstone of effective human-AI collaboration, yet it is fragile and easily eroded. A lack of transparency, the generation of inaccurate or biased outputs, and a perception that the system operates without meaningful human oversight are all significant barriers to trust [3]. Once lost, trust is exceedingly difficult to regain.
- **The Need for Human-Centric Skills**: The AI era demands a new set of "soft skills" that are often undervalued in traditional, engineering-driven organizational

cultures. Skills such as curiosity (the drive to explore and question), resilience (the ability to adapt to chaotic change), tolerance for ambiguity (the capacity to act without complete information), perspective-taking (empathy for other stakeholders), and humility (the willingness to admit uncertainty and defer to others' expertise) are now essential for navigating the complexities of AI implementation [22]. Most organizations are not yet equipped to teach or incentivize these critical human-centric competencies.

The interplay between these challenges creates a complex system of reinforcement. For example, the technical challenge of explainability is directly linked to the organizational challenge of leadership buy-in. A leader presented with an opaque "black box" system is less likely to trust it or invest the significant resources required for its deployment, especially when faced with employee resistance. This lack of leadership demand, in turn, disincentivizes technical teams from prioritizing the development of explainability features, particularly if doing so might compromise raw performance metrics. This creates a vicious cycle where technical limitations fuel organizational inertia, and vice versa. Breaking this cycle requires a strategic intervention from leadership to redefine "performance" to explicitly include transparency and trustworthiness, thereby creating the business case for investing in the technical solutions for explainability. The following table provides a consolidated framework of these challenges and potential mitigation strategies (Table 5.3).

5.2.2 The Ethical Imperative: Embedding Responsibility by Design

Beyond the technical and organizational hurdles, the implementation of GAI carries a profound ethical weight. The potential for these systems to cause harm—by perpetuating bias, violating privacy, spreading misinformation, or damaging the environment—is substantial. A human-centric approach mandates that these ethical considerations are not treated as peripheral compliance issues but are woven into the very fabric of the AI system through a principle known as "ethics by design" [9]. This proactive stance seeks to anticipate and mitigate harm before it occurs, ensuring that the technology aligns with fundamental human rights and societal values.

Addressing Algorithmic Bias and Ensuring Fairness

One of the most persistent and damaging ethical challenges in AI is algorithmic bias. GAI models, trained on vast datasets scraped from the internet and other sources, inevitably absorb and can amplify the societal biases present in that data [23]. This can lead to discriminatory outcomes that reinforce historical inequities. For example, AI systems have been shown to disproportionately flag welfare claims from individuals based on age and disability [3], downgrade the academic assessments of students

Table 5.3 A multi-dimensional framework of HCG-AI implementation challenges

Challenge category	Specific challenge	Key mitigation strategies
Technical	Lack of explainability ("Black Box" problem)	Invest in explainable AI (XAI) research and tools; design interfaces that communicate uncertainty and rationale [3]
	Robustness and reliability (e.g., hallucinations)	Implement rigorous testing and validation protocols; build in "human-in-the-loop" review for high-stakes outputs; design for graceful failure [14]
	Security vulnerabilities (e.g., prompt injection)	Employ adversarial testing ("red teaming") to identify weaknesses; implement input/output filters and content moderation safeguards [16]
Organizational	Resistance to change	Utilize established change management frameworks; ensure clear, consistent communication; involve employees in the implementation process [19]
	Lack of leadership buy-in	Present a clear business case that aligns HCG-AI with strategic objectives and demonstrates ROI beyond pure efficiency (e.g., improved trust, lower risk) [20]
	Workforce disruption and skills gap	Invest heavily in continuous learning, reskilling, and upskilling programs; foster a culture that values both technical and human-centric skills [7]
	Siloed, cross-disciplinary collaboration	Create dedicated, interdisciplinary teams; establish a common vocabulary and shared project goals; foster a culture of psychological safety and mutual respect [3]
Human element	Fear and emotional barriers to adoption	Acknowledge and address concerns transparently; involve stakeholders early and often to build a sense of ownership and control [19]
	Lack of trust	Prioritize transparency, explainability, and user control; ensure meaningful human oversight is always present [3]
	Deficit in human-centric skills	Redefine performance frameworks to include and incentivize skills like curiosity, empathy, and humility; integrate coaching on these skills into AI training [22]

from disadvantaged backgrounds [24], and recommend higher loan denial rates for minority groups [25].

An "ethics by design" approach confronts this challenge head-on. It requires that fairness be a primary design constraint, not an afterthought. This involves several key practices [11, 26]. Addressing algorithmic bias in generative AI requires a multi-faceted approach that begins at the very foundation of model development: Data

Curation and Auditing. Because AI models learn from historical datasets that often mirror societal prejudices, developers must rigorously audit training data to identify and rectify imbalances. This process involves more than just removing overtly harmful content; it necessitates a proactive strategy to seek out and integrate data from underrepresented groups, ensuring that the resulting model reflects a global and diverse reality rather than a narrow or skewed perspective. By curating data that is as representative as possible, the "ground truth" the AI learns from is anchored in inclusivity, which significantly reduces the likelihood of the system producing exclusionary or stereotypical outputs.

To complement these technical audits, organizations must prioritize the assembly of diverse review teams. Technical expertise alone is often insufficient to detect the subtle, nuanced ways that bias can manifest in AI-generated text, images, or code. By forming interdisciplinary teams—comprising ethicists, sociologists, and individuals from various cultural, racial, and socioeconomic backgrounds—developers can leverage a broader range of "lived experience" to scrutinize model outputs. These diverse perspectives act as a critical safety net, identifying blind spots and potential harms that a more homogenous group of engineers might overlook. This human-led oversight is not a one-time event but is sustained through regular bias assessments. These protocols involve continuous testing and monitoring throughout the model's entire lifecycle, from pre-training to post-deployment. As the model interacts with the real world, its behavior may shift; therefore, ongoing measurement is essential to ensure that fairness remains a permanent feature rather than an initial afterthought.

Finally, when biases are identified, sophisticated mitigation techniques must be applied to the model's architecture and training process. This includes technical interventions such as re-weighting training data to give more prominence to underrepresented examples or employing adversarial debiasing, where a secondary "adversary" model is used to challenge the primary system whenever it relies on biased correlations. Furthermore, developers can bake fairness constraints directly into the model's objective function during the training phase, essentially teaching the AI that accuracy is inseparable from equity. These structural interventions, combined with human-centric auditing and diverse oversight, create a robust defense against the propagation of systemic bias, transforming GAI into a more equitable and trustworthy tool for all users.

Safeguarding Privacy and Data Protection in the Age of LLMs

The voracious appetite of LLMs for data creates unprecedented challenges for privacy and data protection [2]. These models are often trained on petabytes of text and image data, which can include sensitive personal information, proprietary corporate data, and copyrighted material. The risk of this data being inadvertently memorized and reproduced by the model, or misused in other ways, is significant.

A human-centric approach to GAI must therefore be grounded in robust data governance and a deep respect for privacy. This includes the following:

- **Adherence to Regulations**: Strict compliance with data protection laws such as the General Data Protection Regulation (GDPR) in Europe and the California Consumer Privacy Act (CCPA) is a baseline requirement [11].
- **Data Ownership and Consent**: Upholding the principle that individuals and organizations own their data and the insights derived from it [27]. This means obtaining explicit and informed consent for data use and being transparent about how data is collected, stored, and processed [12].
- **Privacy-Preserving Techniques**: Employing technical safeguards such as data anonymization, differential privacy, and secure data management protocols to minimize the risk of exposing sensitive information [13].

Navigating Intellectual Property and Combating Misinformation

GAI fundamentally challenges traditional concepts of authorship, originality, and intellectual property (IP) [11]. When a model generates an image in the style of a living artist or produces text based on copyrighted books, questions of ownership and fair use become legally and ethically complex [28]. Navigating this landscape requires clear policies, documentation of data sources, and careful review of outputs for potential IP conflicts [11].

Simultaneously, the ease with which GAI can generate convincing but false content poses a severe threat to the information ecosystem. The potential for GAI to be used to create and disseminate misinformation, disinformation, and malicious "deep fakes" on a massive scale is a critical societal risk [11]. Mitigating this requires a multi-pronged strategy [11, 13].

Maintaining the integrity of the digital information ecosystem requires a robust commitment to content verification and authentication. This process involves the implementation of rigorous fact-checking protocols that go beyond traditional methods to address the specific nuances of AI-generated misinformation. A key technical pillar in this effort is the use of authentication tools such as digital watermarking—for example, technologies like SynthID—which embed imperceptible markers directly into the pixels of an image or the metadata of a document. Furthermore, provenance tracking (such as the C2PA standard) provides a transparent "chain of custody" for digital assets, allowing users and platforms to verify the origin of a piece of media and distinguish between authentic human-created content and synthetic outputs. By establishing these technical baselines, organizations can create a more resilient information environment where the source and history of content are verifiable by default.

Complementing these technical safeguards is the necessity for transparency and disclosure. Ethical GAI deployment mandates that users are clearly informed when they are interacting with an AI system or viewing content synthesized by one. This transparency is crucial for managing user expectations and fostering a healthy level of skepticism; when content is explicitly labeled as AI-generated, it encourages individuals to apply critical evaluation to the information presented. Whether through clear UI labeling, verbal disclosures in audio interfaces, or visible tags on social media platforms, providing this context prevents the unintentional blurring of reality and ensures that the "liar's dividend"—the ability for bad actors to dismiss real events as "AI-generated"—is minimized.

Finally, the ethical landscape must be fortified by prohibiting deceptive use through the establishment of clear, enforceable guidelines. These frameworks must explicitly forbid the use of GAI for malicious purposes, such as the creation of fraudulent reviews, the mass production of disinformation campaigns, or the development of deepfakes intended to manipulate individuals against their best interests. By defining these red lines, developers and policymakers can move toward a governance model that prioritizes the public good over engagement metrics. Prohibiting deceptive use is not merely about preventing technical misuse; it is about protecting the fundamental trust that allows a society to function, ensuring that GAI remains a tool for empowerment rather than a mechanism for large-scale psychological or social manipulation.

The Environmental and Societal Footprint of GAI

The ethical considerations of GAI extend beyond data and algorithms to its physical impact on the world. The computational power required to train and deploy large-scale GAI models is immense, leading to significant environmental costs. Data centers consume staggering amounts of electricity and water for cooling, placing a strain on power grids and local ecosystems [29]. For example, global data center electricity consumption was estimated at 460 terawatt-hours in 2022 and is projected to approach 1,050 terawatt-hours by 2026 [29]. This environmental footprint is an often-overlooked ethical dimension of GAI development [11].

Furthermore, if access to powerful GAI tools is limited to affluent individuals, corporations, or nations, it risks widening the existing digital divide and exacerbating global inequalities [24]. This aligns with the UNESCO principle of sustainability, which asserts that AI systems should benefit all human beings, including future generations, and must be evaluated for their broad social and environmental impacts [30].

These ethical challenges are not isolated issues but are deeply interconnected, creating a complex "ethical entanglement." For instance, the effort to mitigate algorithmic bias by collecting more diverse and representative data can run directly into conflict with the principle of data privacy. Similarly, attempts to combat misinformation with powerful content filters may themselves introduce biases, unfairly censoring certain viewpoints or communities. Respecting intellectual property by training models on more limited, licensed datasets could inadvertently reduce the diversity of the training data, potentially increasing the risk of bias. This reveals that implementing ethical GAI is rarely about finding a perfect technical fix. Instead, it is about navigating difficult trade-offs between competing values. This reality underscores the critical need for robust, multi-stakeholder governance structures—such as the AI Ethics Boards and advisory panels proposed by organizations like IBM and

SAP [9]—that can deliberate on these value-laden decisions and establish context-specific policies. The solution is ultimately procedural and organizational, not just algorithmic.

5.3 Human-Centric Generative AI in Practice: Sector-Specific Scenarios

To move beyond theoretical frameworks and abstract challenges, it is essential to examine how human-centric generative AI is being implemented in real-world contexts. By analyzing specific case studies from diverse sectors—healthcare, education, and customer engagement—we can distill practical lessons about what works, what the challenges are, and how human-centric principles translate into tangible outcomes. These scenarios demonstrate that HCG-AI is not a monolithic concept but a flexible philosophy that adapts to the unique needs and ethical considerations of each domain.

5.3.1 Transforming Healthcare: Augmenting Compassion and Precision

The healthcare sector, with its high-stakes decisions and deeply human focus, presents both a significant opportunity and a profound responsibility for HCG-AI. Implementations in this field must balance the drive for clinical precision and efficiency with the core values of patient care, empathy, and trust.

Case Study Analysis: User-Centered Deployment of Clinical AI Tools

A compelling example of HCG-AI in practice is the deployment of **expanse navigator**, an AI-powered search and summarization tool developed by Google and MEDITECH for integration within electronic health record (EHR) systems [31]. The tool is designed to provide clinicians with a comprehensive, AI-generated view of a patient's health history, making critical data more accessible.

The implementation at Mile Bluff Medical Center was guided by a robust, user-centered research program that engaged 128 healthcare professionals across 24 departments. This program was not an afterthought but a core part of the deployment strategy, consisting of four key components:

1. **Naturalistic Observation**: Researchers observed clinicians in their natural workflows *before* deployment to understand existing pain points and build rapport.

2. **Pre- and Post-deployment Surveys**: Quantitative data was collected on user satisfaction, perceived helpfulness, and time savings, establishing a clear baseline for comparison.
3. **Early Integration Product Testing**: A small group of users tested the integrated product on structured tasks, providing immediate feedback that informed user onboarding and training materials.
4. **In-depth User Interviews**: Qualitative interviews were conducted post-launch to capture nuanced experiences and identify high-value use cases [31].

This deeply collaborative, mixed-methods approach yielded remarkable results. Post-deployment, 86% of respondents reported high satisfaction, 91% felt the AI system was faster than the baseline, and adoption was high, with 93% of eligible staff accessing the tool within 3 months. The study concluded that this user-centered framework was not only feasible but highly effective for deploying clinical AI, underscoring the value of close collaboration, rapid feedback incorporation, and tailored user training [31].

Enhancing Doctor-Patient Communication and Scaling Empathy

Beyond clinical efficiency, HCG-AI is being explored as a tool to augment the human side of medicine. The administrative burden on physicians often leads to burnout and can detract from meaningful patient interaction. GAI offers a potential solution by automating routine tasks while enhancing the quality of communication.

A recent study from NYU found that AI-generated responses to patient messages were rated by a panel of healthcare professionals as significantly more empathetic than those written by physicians themselves [32]. The AI replies scored higher on warmth, tone, and relational language. While the physicians' responses were sometimes more clinically precise, the AI excelled at conveying positivity and building connection. This suggests a powerful collaborative model: GAI can draft empathetic, personalized responses, relieving the cognitive load on doctors and freeing them to focus on complex clinical judgments, while still ensuring a culture of compassion is maintained and even scaled [32].

This "human-in-the-loop" model is being put into practice. A collaboration between Duke Health and NTT DATA is developing a home-care model for cancer patients that uses a GenAI-driven virtual agent to handle routine monitoring and communication. Crucially, the system is designed to keep medical staff in direct contact with the patient, ensuring a human is always overseeing the care and can intervene when necessary. This approach aims to provide high-value care in a more comfortable setting for the patient, powered by AI but guided by human expertise [33].

Accelerating Drug Discovery and Personalized Medicine

The impact of HCG-AI in healthcare extends to backend scientific research, where it can analyze complex biological data at a scale and speed far beyond human capabilities. GAI algorithms can explore and analyze vast datasets to discover new patterns and trends, significantly accelerating the drug discovery process [34]. AI-driven protein structure predictions and molecule generation can shorten the development lifecycle for new treatments, potentially bringing life-saving therapies to market faster and at a lower cost [35].

Furthermore, GAI is a key enabler of personalized medicine. By analyzing a patient's unique genomic data, lifestyle factors, and ongoing health information, AI systems can help create customized care plans and treatment regimens. This moves medicine away from a one-size-fits-all approach toward highly tailored interventions that can improve patient outcomes and reduce adverse effects [35]. In these applications, the "human-centric" aspect is realized not through direct user interaction, but by directing the power of AI toward the fundamental human goal of improving health and well-being.

5.3.2 Revolutionizing Education: Personalization, Equity, and Critical Thinking

In the field of education, GAI has been met with both excitement for its potential to personalize learning and apprehension about its potential to enable academic dishonesty. A human-centric approach seeks to harness the former while mitigating the latter, reframing GAI not as a threat to be policed, but as a powerful pedagogical tool that can enhance engagement, equity, and, most importantly, critical thinking.

Case Study Analysis: The Human-Centric AI-First (HCAIF) Teaching Framework

The Newcastle Business School at the University of Newcastle in Australia has developed and implemented a comprehensive human-centric AI-first (HCAIF) framework for a new undergraduate program in innovation and entrepreneurship [36]. This framework, developed after 20 months of research, is built on five pillars that integrate GAI into the entire learning process.

The evolution of the modern classroom begins with a collaborative preparation phase, where teachers leverage generative AI as a sophisticated design partner. Instead of relying on static curricula, educators work alongside AI to build dynamic repositories of learning resources, tailored exercises, and multifaceted assessments that can adapt to varying skill levels. This synergy allows for a transition into a highly personalized learning environment, where students utilize GAI tools for deep research, creative content generation, and rapid prototyping. Within this framework, students receive immediate, individualized feedback from the AI, which acts as a constant academic scaffold. This automated support is strategically balanced by structured peer review sessions, ensuring that while the technology accelerates technical output, the human elements of critical critique and social learning remain central to the educational experience.

During active classroom hours, the physical learning space is transformed into an immersive environment focused on high-level engagement. With the AI handling routine information delivery and initial feedback, the teacher's role shifts from a primary lecturer to an expert coach and facilitator. In this setting, educators lead teamwork exercises and complex discussions while the AI provides real-time analytical insights, such as performing sentiment analysis on a student's sales pitch or tracking the logic flow in a live debate. This allows the teacher to intervene at precisely the right moment with the nuanced guidance that only a human mentor can provide.

The cycle of learning concludes with a balanced approach to summative assessment and long-term progress monitoring. While AI tools are employed to generate complex testing materials and provide preliminary grading—vastly reducing the administrative burden on staff—the teacher retains absolute oversight to ensure every evaluation aligns with rigorous academic standards and remains free of algorithmic error. Furthermore, AI-driven monitoring tools track student progress in real-time, visualizing learning gaps and performance trends through comprehensive dashboards. By identifying struggling students the moment they begin to veer off track, these systems empower teachers to provide targeted, empathetic support exactly when it is needed most, ensuring that no student is left behind in a data-driven educational landscape.

This case study demonstrates a balanced and thoughtful integration of AI. It leverages the technology for personalization and efficiency while keeping the human educator firmly in the role of coach, mentor, and facilitator of critical thinking [36].

GAI for Adaptive Learning Pathways and Inclusive Content Creation

The HCAIF framework is one example of a broader movement to use GAI to create more adaptive and equitable learning experiences. GAI-powered tools can create personalized curricula by analyzing individual student performance data, adjusting the difficulty of questions in real-time, and offering multiple ways to explain complex concepts [37].

Virtual tutoring systems, such as Khan Academy's Khanmigo, which is built on GPT-4, act as Socratic guides, helping students solve problems step-by-step rather than simply providing answers. This encourages critical thinking and self-discovery [37]. Other tools, like Quizlet's Q-Chat, use GAI to create interactive, conversational quizzes that provide real-time feedback.

This technology also holds immense potential for expanding accessibility. GAI can help bridge educational gaps by providing high-quality learning resources to students in resource-constrained environments [24]. It can also create content that is more inclusive, for example, by generating learning materials that are sensitive to diverse linguistic and cultural backgrounds, thereby helping to address inequities that marginalized groups often face [24].

Balancing AI Tools with Human Pedagogy: Attribution and Reflection

A critical innovation of the HCAIF framework, and a cornerstone of a human-centric approach in education, is its explicit focus on metacognition—teaching students how to think about their own learning process. This is achieved through two essential requirements [36]: Attribution and reflection.

The integration of generative AI (GAI) into the academic workflow requires a fundamental shift in how we define authorship and integrity. Rather than treating AI as a "shortcut" to be concealed, the practice of attribution reframes it as a transparent component of the scholarly process. This shift demands that students provide granular documentation—essentially a "process trace"—of how and where GAI was utilized. By citing specific prompts, iterative refinements, and the specific sections of a project influenced by synthetic output, the use of AI moves from a hidden activity into the light of academic discourse.

For educators, this transparency is transformative; it allows them to look "under the hood" of a final submission to evaluate a student's problem-solving capabilities and co-creation proficiency. Instead of grading a static end-product, instructors can assess how a student navigated the tool's limitations, corrected its hallucinations, and directed its creative potential. This approach ensures that the "human in the loop" remains the primary architect of the work, demonstrating critical thinking through the sophisticated management of technological resources.

Complementing this transparency is the requirement for deep reflection, typically facilitated through structured journaling. In these journals, students are tasked with performing a meta-cognitive analysis of their relationship with the technology. They must critically examine why they chose to use GAI for a specific task—such as summarizing a dense text or generating code—and evaluate the tool's effectiveness versus its failures.

By analyzing the broader impact of AI on their own learning curves, students transition from being passive consumers of content to becoming critical evaluators of logic and style. These reflective practices force students to confront the "black box" of AI, asking difficult questions about its biases, its tendency toward genericism, and its impact on their own voice. Ultimately, this habit of reflection ensures that students do not outsource their thinking, but rather use the technology as a mirror to better understand their own intellectual strengths and areas for growth.

By mandating attribution and reflection, this pedagogical model successfully reframes GAI. It ceases to be merely a tool for completing assignments and becomes an object of study in itself. Students learn to leverage its power while remaining critical of its weaknesses, thereby developing the essential skills of ethical and effective engagement with AI that will be paramount in their future careers.

5.3.3 Augmenting Creativity and Customer Engagement

In the commercial sphere, HCG-AI is reshaping how businesses interact with their customers and how creative professionals approach their craft. The focus is on using GAI to enhance human connection, personalize experiences, and free up human talent to focus on higher-value, uniquely human tasks like strategic thinking, emotional engagement, and conceptual innovation.

GAI as a Collaborative Partner in the Creative Industries

The creative industries are undergoing a profound transformation, with GAI emerging as a powerful collaborative partner. Rather than replacing human artists, GAI is being used to augment the creative process in several ways:

- **Visual Arts**: Platforms like **DALL-E** and **Midjourney** allow artists to rapidly generate visual concepts, explore novel styles, and automate time-consuming tasks like background removal or color correction. This frees the artist to concentrate on the conceptual and emotional core of their work [28].
- **Music**: AI tools can assist with composition by generating original musical phrases, suggesting harmonic progressions, or creating new instrumental layers for a remix. This democratizes music production and serves as a source of inspiration for human composers, who retain final creative control [38].
- **Writing**: AI-powered writing assistants can generate drafts, summarize research, or suggest headlines, accelerating the content creation process. This allows human writers to focus on in-depth analysis, nuanced storytelling, and adding the cultural context and emotional depth that AI cannot replicate [28].

In this symbiotic model, human capital remains the wellspring of originality and judgment. The value of human creativity—personal stories, emotional resonance, and cultural nuance—is preserved and even enhanced, as GAI handles the more mechanical aspects of creation [38].

Case Study Analysis: Enhancing Customer Service with GAI

Several leading companies have successfully implemented HCG-AI to transform their customer service operations, demonstrating that automation and human connection are not mutually exclusive goals.

- **Verizon**: The telecommunications giant implemented a GAI-powered assistant, trained on thousands of internal documents, to help its customer service agents answer queries more efficiently. The AI suggests context-based answers, allowing agents to resolve 95% of queries with greater speed and accuracy. This efficiency gain did not lead to layoffs; instead, Verizon reskilled its customer care agents into sales specialists, freeing them up to focus on higher-value, relationship-building interactions. The result was a 40% increase in sales, demonstrating a successful human-AI collaboration that drove business value while empowering employees [39].

- **ING**: The Dutch multinational bank faced the challenge of high query volumes and the need for 24/7 support. They deployed a conversational AI assistant, but with strict human-centric guardrails. Risk stakeholders were involved from the beginning, a "human-in-the-loop" system was established to handle low-confidence AI responses, and the AI was restricted from giving advice on sensitive financial topics. This focus on trust and safety allowed ING to serve 20% more customers within the first seven weeks of the pilot, improving customer satisfaction while maintaining the bank's reputation for reliability [39].
- **United Airlines**: The airline enhanced its existing "every flight has a story" initiative with GAI. This program provides customers with detailed, empathetic explanations for flight delays. Previously, this was a manual process. By using GAI to draft these narratives from operational data, United was able to scale the initiative from 15% of delayed flights to a target of 50%. Crucially, human "storytellers" still review and approve the messages, ensuring they maintain a human, empathetic tone. This human-AI partnership led to a 6% increase in customer satisfaction, turning a negative experience (a delay) into an opportunity to build trust through transparent communication [39].

Human-in-the-Loop Models in Professional Services

The "humans + AI" model is becoming a dominant paradigm in professional services, where deep expertise and nuanced judgment are paramount. Firms are integrating GAI into their workflows not to replace professionals, but to make them faster, more accurate, and more efficient.

For example, law firms are using GAI tools that can draft and red-line contracts against pre-defined playbooks in minutes, a process that would typically take hours. The AI heat-maps potential risk areas and flags non-standard clauses. However, the final decision-making power remains firmly in human hands. Deal lawyers set the initial risk parameters, review the AI's mark-ups, and partners provide the final sign-off on any flagged issues. This workflow can cut contract cycle times by 50–70%, allowing lawyers to focus their expertise on strategic negotiation and complex legal reasoning rather than on tedious document review [40]. This model of AI-powered drafting followed by senior human assurance is being replicated across consulting, finance, and auditing, showcasing a scalable and effective structure for human-AI collaboration in knowledge-intensive industries [40].

5.4 Frameworks for Accountability and a Look Ahead

The successful and responsible implementation of human-centric generative AI requires more than just good intentions and well-designed projects; it demands robust frameworks for accountability. This involves establishing clear, comprehensive metrics to evaluate human-centricity, creating actionable guidelines for all stakeholders, and engaging with the broader policy landscape to shape a future where AI serves human interests. This final part synthesizes the report's findings into these actionable frameworks and offers a critical perspective on the path ahead.

5.4.1 Evaluating Human-Centricity: Metrics and Methodologies

Evaluating an HCG-AI system requires moving beyond traditional technical metrics like latency or accuracy. The assessment must be holistic, capturing the quality of the user experience, the fairness of the system's outcomes, and its alignment with ethical principles. This requires a combination of quantitative and qualitative methodologies.

Frameworks for Assessing User Experience and Satisfaction

Human evaluation is indispensable for assessing GAI because it can capture subjective qualities that automated metrics miss [15]. The goal is to measure how effectively the AI meets human expectations and delivers a satisfactory experience. Key metrics in this domain include the following:

- **Quality of Output**:
  - **Fluency**: Is the generated content grammatically correct and natural-sounding?
  - **Coherence and Consistency**: Does the output maintain a logical flow and use consistent terminology?
  - **Clarity**: Is the information presented in an easily understandable manner?
  - **Accuracy**: Does the output reflect the intended meaning and is it factually correct [15]?
- **User Interaction and Satisfaction**:
  - **Helpfulness**: Does the AI provide valuable assistance that helps users achieve their goals?
  - **Ease of Use**: Is the system intuitive and straightforward to interact with?
  - **Task Success Rate**: Can users successfully complete their intended tasks using the AI?
  - **Overall User Satisfaction**: How do users rate their overall experience with the system, often measured through surveys or direct feedback [15]?

- **Human-Likeness and Interpretability**:
  - **Human-Likeness**: Does the AI exhibit human-like qualities such as empathy, contextual understanding, or appropriate emotional nuance?
  - **Interpretability**: Can users understand the reasoning behind the AI's decisions or outputs [15]?

Advanced evaluation techniques, such as the use of **adaptive rubrics**, are also emerging. Instead of using a generic rating scale, this method adaptively generates a unique set of pass/fail tests for each individual prompt, ensuring the evaluation is highly relevant to the specific task being assessed. This moves evaluation from subjective scores to granular, objective results, similar to unit testing in software development [41].

Quantitative and Qualitative Metrics for Fairness and Bias Detection

Evaluating the fairness of a GAI system is a critical component of HCG-AI accountability. This involves a dedicated effort to detect and measure systemic bias that could cause harm to certain demographic groups. This evaluation should occur at two stages:

1. **Data Bias Metrics**: Before a model is even trained, the raw data should be analyzed for pre-existing biases. Metrics include the following:
   - **Difference in Population Size**: Are certain demographic groups significantly under- or over-represented in the dataset?
   - **Difference in Positive Proportions in True Labels**: In a labeled dataset, do positive outcomes appear at different rates for different groups [42]?
2. **Model Bias Metrics**: After the model is trained, its predictions must be evaluated for biased outcomes. Key metrics, often calculated by comparing confusion matrices across different demographic slices (e.g., by race, gender, or age), include the following:
   - **Accuracy Difference**: Does the model perform more accurately for one group than another?
   - **Recall Difference**: Does the model have a higher true positive rate for one group?
   - **Difference in Ratio of Error Types**: Does the model make different kinds of mistakes (false positives vs. false negatives) for different groups [42]?

Beyond these statistical measures, two foundational fairness concepts are often used as benchmarks:

- **Demographic Parity**: This metric assesses whether the model's predictions are independent of a sensitive attribute. For example, a loan approval model would satisfy demographic parity if it approves applicants from all racial groups at the same rate [43].

- **Equality of Opportunity**: This metric is less strict, focusing on whether the model performs equally well for individuals who are equally qualified, regardless of their demographic group. For instance, it would require that among all *qualified* loan applicants, the approval rate is the same across all racial groups [43].

It is crucial to recognize that these quantitative metrics alone are insufficient. They must be complemented by qualitative audits, stakeholder engagement with affected communities, and the use of explainability tools to understand the root causes of identified biases [26].

Establishing a Continuous Feedback and Improvement Loop

As established earlier, HCG-AI systems are not static. Therefore, evaluation cannot be a one-time event. A culture of continuous improvement, fueled by robust user feedback, is essential for ensuring the system remains aligned with human needs and values over its entire lifecycle [14].

The realization of an ethical AI framework depends on the seamless integration of accessible feedback channels directly within the application's interface, ensuring that the burden of reporting does not fall heavily on the user. These mechanisms must be designed with high intuitive utility, allowing users to instantly flag biased outputs, technical inaccuracies, or emotionally unsatisfactory experiences as they occur. By providing a transparent and frictionless pathway for communication, developers can gather a rich repository of qualitative data that reflects the diverse lived experiences of their user base, which is essential for identifying edge cases that automated testing might overlook. This continuous stream of information is then funned into a structured regimen of regular performance reviews, which serve as a critical governance checkpoint. Unlike traditional technical audits that prioritize computational efficiency, these reviews must explicitly utilize human-centric metrics—such as fairness, user autonomy, and psychological well-being—to assess whether the system remains aligned with its original ethical mandates.

To bridge the gap between identifying issues and implementing solutions, organizations must cultivate a culture of continuous learning and institutional curiosity. This involves more than just technical upskilling; it requires a fundamental shift where development teams are encouraged to treat feedback as a primary driver of innovation rather than a record of failure. By staying actively engaged with the latest advancements in AI ethics and human–computer interaction research, engineers and product managers can proactively adapt to shifting societal norms and emerging regulatory requirements. This holistic approach ensures that the AI system is not a static product, but a dynamic entity that evolves through a virtuous cycle of user engagement, rigorous self-assessment, and an organizational commitment to the public good.

The following table provides a consolidated compendium of these evaluation metrics, offering a practical toolkit for organizations (Table 5.4).

Table 5.4 A compendium of human-centric evaluation metrics

Evaluation domain	Metric	Description	Methodology
User experience	Task success rate	The percentage of users who successfully complete a defined task using the AI system	Usability testing, user surveys [15]
	User satisfaction (CSAT/NPS)	A measure of users' overall satisfaction with their interaction with the AI	Surveys, In-app Feedback [15]
	Fluency & Coherence	The grammatical correctness, naturalness, and logical flow of generated text	Human Evaluation Panels [15]
	Helpfulness and relevance	The degree to which the AI's output assists the user and is relevant to their query	Human evaluation, A/B testing [15]
Fairness and bias	Demographic parity	Measures whether the rate of positive outcomes is equal across different demographic groups	Statistical analysis of model outputs [43]
	Equality of opportunity	Measures whether the true positive rate is equal across different demographic groups	Statistical analysis of model outputs [43]
	Accuracy difference	The difference in model accuracy between various demographic subgroups	Statistical analysis of model outputs [42]
Ethical and safety	Toxicity score	A measure of the presence of harmful, offensive, or inappropriate content in the AI's output	Automated classifiers, human review [16]
	Explainability rating	A qualitative assessment of how well users can understand the AI's reasoning	User interviews, surveys [15]
	Data privacy compliance	An audit to ensure the system adheres to data protection regulations (e.g., GDPR)	Legal and compliance review [12]

5.4.2 A Blueprint for Responsible Implementation

Building on the lifecycle, challenges, and evaluation frameworks, this section synthesizes the report's findings into a clear blueprint for responsible HCG-AI implementation. This involves distinct but overlapping guidelines for the key actors within an organization, as well as an engagement with the broader ecosystem of governance and policy.

Actionable Guidelines for Developers, Designers, and Organizational Leaders

Responsible implementation is a shared responsibility, requiring a coordinated effort from all stakeholders.

- **For Developers and Designers**:
  - **Prioritize Usability from Day One**: Treat user experience not as a final polish but as a foundational requirement. Involve users throughout the design process through interviews, co-creation workshops, and continuous usability testing [10].
  - **Design for Failure and Transparency**: Proactively anticipate potential system errors and design graceful failure modes that provide users with clear feedback. Be transparent about the AI's capabilities and limitations, and clearly disclose when and how data is being used [14].
  - **Embed Ethics in the Workflow**: Use bias detection tools and diverse datasets during development. Conduct proactive risk assessments to identify potential harms and build in safeguards. Be explicit about where human review and intervention are necessary [13].
- **For Organizational Leaders**:
  - **Champion a Human-Centric Vision**: Leadership buy-in is critical. Leaders must articulate a clear vision for AI that prioritizes human well-being alongside business objectives, adopting a "double bottom line" approach [7].
  - **Give Ethics a Seat at the Table**: Move beyond performative "ethics washing." Establish an empowered, well-funded AI ethics committee or officer with genuine authority to guide and, if necessary, halt projects that do not meet ethical standards [9].
  - **Foster a Culture of Learning and Psychological Safety**: Invest heavily in reskilling and upskilling the workforce for an AI-augmented future. Create an environment where employees feel safe to experiment, provide feedback, and question AI outputs without fear of reprisal [44].

- **Demand and Document Accountability**: Establish clear governance structures and hold individuals and teams accountable for the ethical implementation of AI. Create a culture of documentation to ensure that AI use cases, data sources, and governance decisions are traceable and transparent [45].

The Role of Governance, Policy, and International Standards

While organizational action is essential, the scale and impact of GAI necessitate a broader framework of public governance and international cooperation. A purely self-regulatory approach is insufficient to address the profound societal implications of this technology.

Key policy recommendations emerging from international bodies like UNESCO and the OECD provide a roadmap for governments [46]: To ensure that technological progress does not bypass ethical boundaries, regulations must prioritize the definition and maintenance of meaningful human control. This requires that AI systems be intentionally engineered as assistive tools that augment human decision-making rather than acting as autonomous replacements for human judgment. By establishing that the ultimate responsibility and legal accountability for any AI-driven outcome must always reside with human actors, society can prevent the erosion of agency and the emergence of accountability gaps. This principle of control is deeply intertwined with the necessity for absolute transparency and explainability. Public policy should mandate that AI systems, especially those deployed in high-stakes public sector areas like law enforcement, healthcare, or social services, are fully interpretable. Those impacted by automated decisions have a fundamental right to understand the logic behind those choices, ensuring that systems are not "black boxes" but are instead open to scrutiny and corrective action.

Furthermore, the successful integration of AI into society requires a proactive governmental commitment to promoting AI literacy and fostering inclusive deliberation. It is essential for the state to invest in public education initiatives that build a digitally literate citizenry, empowering individuals to participate meaningfully in complex discussions regarding the future of technology. Such governance cannot be handled by industry experts alone; it demands a comprehensive multi-stakeholder approach that actively integrates perspectives from civil society, academia, and marginalized communities who are often most vulnerable to algorithmic harm. By anchoring all AI governance within a robust human rights framework, developers and policymakers can ensure that these powerful technologies are deployed in a manner that respects inherent dignity and promotes fairness, justice, and environmental sustainability. This holistic approach transforms AI from a purely technical pursuit into a societal endeavor dedicated to the protection and advancement of fundamental human values.

5.4.3 *The Future of Human-AI Symbiosis*

The future of human-AI symbiosis represents a pivotal juncture in the history of human innovation, marking a transition from using tools for task execution to collaborating with autonomous cognitive partners. As we stand at the precipice of this new technological era, it is increasingly clear that the trajectory of generative AI is not a fixed path determined by the capabilities of the code alone, but is a socially constructed journey. The strategic choices made today by researchers in algorithmic design, by corporations in their pursuit of market dominance, and by policymakers in their creation of regulatory guardrails will ultimately determine the character of our shared future. We face a fundamental fork in the road: one path leads toward a future of augmented human potential, where AI acts as a "bicycle for the mind," amplifying our creative capacities and enabling us to solve intractable global challenges like climate change and disease.

Conversely, the alternative path presents a future defined by exacerbated inequality, where the benefits of AI are concentrated among a small elite while the majority of the global population faces diminished agency and economic displacement. A critical assessment of the current landscape reveals a complex tension between these two outcomes. While the promise of GAI offers unprecedented access to knowledge and specialized skills, the peril lies in the potential for these systems to be deployed without sufficient ethical oversight, leading to the erosion of truth and the deepening of social divides. Therefore, the realization of a beneficial symbiosis depends on our collective ability to move beyond passive observation and actively steer technological development toward a human-centric model—one that prioritizes transparency, inclusivity, and the preservation of human dignity above all else.

A Critical Assessment of the Current GAI Landscape

The current GAI landscape is characterized by a stark paradox. On one hand, the pace of technological advancement and investment is staggering. AI performance on complex benchmarks continues to improve dramatically, and business adoption is accelerating, with record levels of private investment fueling a "gold rush" mentality [47]. Research increasingly confirms that AI can deliver significant productivity boosts [47].

On the other hand, this rapid, often profit-driven, development is outpacing our collective ability to understand and shape its societal impact [48]. The responsible AI ecosystem is evolving unevenly; while governments are showing increased urgency in developing governance frameworks, standardized ethical evaluations remain rare among major industry developers, and a gap persists between recognizing risks and taking meaningful action [47]. The dominant narrative is often shaped by utopian visions of productivity and dystopian fears of obsolescence, a polarized discourse that neglects the nuanced and pragmatic ways GAI will actually manifest in society [49]. There is a pressing concern that, without deliberate intervention, the evolution of AI will continue to be driven primarily by the optimization of profits and social control rather than a genuine commitment to the public good [50].

To reconcile these opposing forces, a fundamental realignment of the AI development lifecycle is required, moving beyond abstract principles toward operationalized accountability. Closing the gap between technical capability and societal safety necessitates a transition to a model of radical transparency, where data provenance, environmental footprints, and algorithmic biases are subject to rigorous, independent auditing before deployment. Furthermore, the creation of a multilateral governance framework is essential to prevent a "race to the bottom" in safety standards, ensuring that competitive pressures do not override the public interest. By fostering a collaborative ecosystem that integrates voices from civil society, labor organizations, and the Global South, the trajectory of GAI can be steered away from narrow optimization and toward the fulfillment of human-centric objectives. Only through such deliberate, structural interventions can we transform GAI from a source of systemic unpredictability into a reliable engine for equitable progress.

Emerging Ethical Dilemmas and Long-Term Societal Implications

Looking ahead, the integration of GAI into the fabric of society will surface new and more complex ethical dilemmas. These include fundamental questions about legal personhood and liability when autonomous systems cause harm, the nature of creativity and ownership in a world of AI-generated art, and the potential for AI to be used to emotionally manipulate users on a massive scale [51].

The long-term societal implications are profound and contingent on the choices we make now. If not governed responsibly, GAI risks amplifying harmful stereotypes, widening the digital and economic divide, eroding trust in institutions through the proliferation of misinformation, and creating a future of precarious work for many [52]. The environmental cost of unchecked AI development also poses a significant threat to sustainability [29]. However, a different future is possible. If we can successfully embed human-centric principles into the technology's DNA, GAI has the potential to foster a more inclusive and equitable society, where more cultures and languages are represented, where education and healthcare are more accessible, and where human creativity is unlocked to solve some of the world's most pressing challenges [52].

Navigating this path requires a shift from reactive policy-making to a proactive, multi-stakeholder approach that prioritizes global collaboration. To bridge the gap between systemic risk and transformative potential, international standards must be established to ensure transparency in algorithmic decision-making and provide clear frameworks for accountability. This is not merely a technical challenge, but a socio-technical one; it requires psychologists, ethicists, and community leaders to work alongside computer scientists to define the boundaries of machine influence. By fostering a culture of "ethics by design," the global community can ensure that GAI serves as a tool for individual empowerment rather than a mechanism for surveillance or exclusion. The window of opportunity to shape these norms is narrowing as the technology accelerates, making the alignment of GAI with democratic values and human rights an urgent priority for the decade ahead.

Concluding: Moving from a Technology-First to a Human-First Future

This report has argued for a fundamental shift in the development and deployment of generative AI—a move away from a technology-first paradigm obsessed with capability and automation, toward a human-first philosophy grounded in augmentation, empowerment, and well-being. The ultimate measure of GAI's success will not be the sophistication of its algorithms or the number of tasks it can automate. It will be its demonstrable contribution to human flourishing.

Achieving this vision is not a matter of technical inevitability; it is a matter of conscious and collective choice. It requires architects of these systems—developers, designers, corporate leaders, and policymakers—to embrace a new set of responsibilities. It demands the creation of systems that are transparent by design, fair in their outcomes, and accountable to the people they serve. It necessitates a relentless focus not on what AI *can* do, but on what AI *should* do, for whom, and by what values it should be guided [44]. The path forward lies in architecting a future of genuine human-AI symbiosis, where technology serves not as a replacement for human intelligence, but as its amplifier, partner, and collaborator in the ongoing project of building a more just, creative, and humane world.

References

1. The GenAI Life Cycle—Data Science PM. https://www.datascience-pm.com/the-genai-life-cycle/
2. Human-Centered Generative AI Course | Stanford Online. https://online.stanford.edu/courses/xfm112-human-centered-generative-ai
3. Human Centered AI: Principles, Benefits, Challenges, and Industry.... https://www.tredence.com/blog/human-centered-ai
4. What Is Human-Centered AI (HCAI)?—Updated 2025—The Interaction Design Foundation. https://www.interaction-design.org/literature/topics/human-centered-ai
5. What Is Human-Centered AI?— IBM Research. https://research.ibm.com/blog/what-is-human-centered-ai
6. Human-Centered AI—Human-Computer Interaction Institute. https://www.hcii.cmu.edu/research-areas/human-centered-ai
7. Why Human-Centric Strategies Are Vital in the AI Era—The World Economic Forum. https://www.weforum.org/stories/2025/01/leading-with-purpose-why-human-centric-strategies-are-vital-in-the-ai-era/
8. Generative AI Lifecycle—AWS Documentation. https://docs.aws.amazon.com/wellarchitected/latest/generative-ai-lens/generative-ai-lifecycle.html
9. Handle AI Ethics Dilemmas with Frameworks & Tools. https://research.aimultiple.com/ai-ethics/
10. Human Centered AI: Putting People First in Technology—Omdena. https://www.omdena.com/blog/human-centered-ai-putting-people-first-in-technology

11. Ethical Considerations When Using Generative AI—Magai. https://magai.co/ethical-considerations-when-using-generative-ai/
12. Ethical Standards in Generative Artificial Intelligence | by Borja Garcia Haendler | Medium. https://medium.com/@bghaendler/ethical-standards-in-generative-artificial-intelligence-79b38efacce5
13. Our Human Centric AI Guidelines and Principles. https://multiplai.ai/human-centric-ai-guidelines/
14. Designing for AI: 12 Expert Tips for Human-Centered Design. https://www.softkraft.co/designing-for-ai/
15. Human-Centered AI Evaluation: Best Practices for Accuracy.... https://galileo.ai/blog/human-evaluation-metrics-ai
16. Responsible Generative AI Toolkit | Google AI for Developers—Gemini API. https://ai.google.dev/responsible
17. The Challenges and Opportunities of Human-Centered AI for Trustworthy Robots and Autonomous Systems—ResearchGate. https://www.researchgate.net/publication/351475992_The_Challenges_and_Opportunities_of_Human-Centered_AI_for_Trustworthy_Robots_and_Autonomous_Systems
18. A Practical Guide to Combining Generative AI with Human-Centered Design. https://www.macquarie.com/cz/en/blog/design/a-practical-guide-to-combining-generative-ai-with-human-centered-design.html
19. The People Side of AI: Embracing Technology with a Human-Centric Approach—PwC. https://www.pwc.de/en/digitale-transformation/generative-ai-artificial-intelligence/the-genai-building-blocks/the-people-side-of-ai-embracing-technology-with-a-human-centric-approach.html
20. Obstacles in Human-Centric Organizational Transformation: Navigating the Challenges HR and Business Leaders Face—Mike Horne. https://www.mike-horne.com/blog/obstacles-in-human-centric-organizational-transformation-navigating-the-challenges-hr-and-business-leaders-face
21. AI in HR: How AI Is Transforming the Future of HR | Gartner. https://www.gartner.com/en/human-resources/topics/artificial-intelligence-in-hr
22. 6 Must-Have Human-Centric Skills for the AI Age—Solutions Review. https://solutionsreview.com/must-have-human-centric-skills-for-the-ai-age/
23. What is AI bias? Causes, Effects, and Mitigation Strategies—SAP. https://www.sap.com/resources/what-is-ai-bias
24. 6: Ethical Considerations for GAI in Education: Ensuring a Human-Centered Approach. https://www.emerald.com/books/monograph/17054/chapter/94054335/Ethical-Considerations-for-GAI-in-Education
25. (PDF) Six Human-Centered Artificial Intelligence Grand Challenges—ResearchGate. https://www.researchgate.net/publication/366823036_Six_Human-Centered_Artificial_Intelligence_Grand_Challenges
26. AI Evaluation Metrics—Bias & Fairness—FRANKI T. https://www.francescatabor.com/articles/2025/7/10/ai-evaluation-metrics-bias-amp-fairness
27. What is AI Ethics? | IBM. https://www.ibm.com/think/topics/ai-ethics
28. Generative AI in Creativity: Transforming Creative Industry—Glance AI. https://glance.com/id-ID/blogs/glanceai/ai-trends/generative-ai-in-creativity
29. Explained: Generative AI's Environmental Impact | MIT News. https://news.mit.edu/2025/explained-generative-ai-environmental-impact-0117
30. Ethics of Artificial Intelligence | UNESCO. https://www.unesco.org/en/artificial-intelligence/recommendation-ethics
31. User-Centered Delivery of AI-Powered Health Care Technologies in.... https://humanfactors.jmir.org/2025/1/e76241
32. AI: The Key to Human-Centered Business—I by IMD. https://www.imd.org/ibyimd/artificial-intelligence/ai-the-key-to-human-centered-business/

33. Human-Centric AI in Healthcare | NTT DATA. https://us.nttdata.com/en/engage/power-positive-health-outcomes-in-the-era-of-ai
34. What is Generative AI?—Gen AI Explained—AWS—Updated 2025. https://aws.amazon.com/what-is/generative-ai/
35. Generative AI in Healthcare: Use Cases, Benefits, Challenges of GenAI and Trends 2025. https://www.johnsnowlabs.com/generative-ai-healthcare/
36. A Framework for Human-Centric AI-First Teaching | AACSB. https://www.aacsb.edu/insights/articles/2025/02/a-framework-for-human-centric-ai-first-teaching
37. Top 10 Use Cases of Generative AI in Education—Research AIMultiple. https://research.aimultiple.com/generative-ai-in-education/
38. The Intersection of AI and Human Capital in Creative Industries—HRTech Series. https://techrseries.com/featured/the-intersection-of-ai-and-human-capital-in-creative-industries/
39. What are the Results from GenAI in Customer Service? Case Studies.... https://econsultancy.com/genai-customer-service-results-verizon-ing-united-airlines/
40. Case Studies: Humans + AI in Professional Services. https://humansplus.ai/insights/10-case-studies-humans-ai-in-professional-services/
41. Gen AI Evaluation Service Overview | Generative AI on Vertex AI—Google Cloud. https://cloud.google.com/vertex-ai/generative-ai/docs/models/evaluation-overview
42. Introduction to Model Evaluation for Fairness | Vertex AI—Google Cloud. https://cloud.google.com/vertex-ai/docs/evaluation/intro-evaluation-fairness
43. Fairness: Evaluating for Bias | Machine Learning | Google for.... https://developers.google.com/machine-learning/crash-course/fairness/evaluating-for-bias
44. An Introduction to AI Policy: Prioritizing Human-Centric AI—Solutions Review. https://solutionsreview.com/an-introduction-to-ai-policy-prioritizing-human-centric-ai/
45. The CEO's Guide to Generative AI: Responsible AI & Ethics | IBM. https://www.ibm.com/thought-leadership/institute-business-value/en-us/report/ceo-generative-ai/responsible-ai-ethics
46. Human-Centric AI: From Principles to Actionable and Shared Policies. https://www.global-solutions-initiative.org/publication/human-centric-ai-from-principles-to-actionable-and-shared-policies/
47. The 2025 AI Index Report | Stanford HAI. https://hai.stanford.edu/ai-index/2025-ai-index-report
48. Generative AI, the American Worker, and the Future of Work | Brookings. https://www.brookings.edu/articles/generative-ai-the-american-worker-and-the-future-of-work/
49. The Societal Impacts of Generative Artificial Intelligence: A Balanced Perspective. https://aisel.aisnet.org/jais/vol25/iss1/14/
50. Survey XII: What Is the Future of Ethical AI Design? | Imagining the Internet—Elon University. https://www.elon.edu/u/imagining/surveys/xii-2021/ethical-ai-design-2030/
51. The Ethics of Artificial Intelligence: Issues and Initiatives—European Parliament. https://www.europarl.europa.eu/RegData/etudes/STUD/2020/634452/EPRS_STU(2020)634452_EN.pdf
52. Societal Impact of Generative AI | Michigan Online. https://online.umich.edu/collections/artificial-intelligence/short/societal-impact-of-generative-ai-/

Chapter 6
The Future of Human-Centric Generative AI

The chapter on The Future of Human-Centric Generative AI explores the evolving landscape of generative AI and its potential to significantly impact society in the coming years. It envisions a future where AI systems are increasingly aligned with human values, ethics, and needs, with advances in transparency, explainability, and fairness embedded in the technology's design. The chapter discusses emerging trends such as AI's role in enhancing human creativity, personalizing experiences, and augmenting decision-making processes across various industries. However, it also anticipates new ethical challenges, including the need to address deepening concerns about privacy, data sovereignty, and the social consequences of automation. The future of human-centric generative AI will depend on interdisciplinary collaboration, continuous ethical reflection, and the development of global regulatory frameworks that ensure equitable access and responsible use. Ultimately, the chapter highlights the importance of fostering a balanced, inclusive, and sustainable approach to AI innovation, ensuring that its benefits are widely shared while minimizing harm.

6.1 Introduction

The rocket growth of generative AI technologies has started reforming the society. It has completely changed various sectors such as creative industries, healthcare, and education. The discussion on future of human-centric generative AI does not only cover its technological capabilities but also includes human values, ethics, and societal importance. This chapter presents the developments and challenges to reform the future of generative AI-based systems focusing on a human-centered approach.

The previous chapters discussed the basic principles including fairness, transparency, accountability, privacy, and inclusivity. This chapter aims to give some glimpses on comprehensive analysis for the future of generative AI. This chapter also

T. Hazra et al., *Building Human-Centered Generative AI*,
https://doi.org/10.1007/978-3-032-21412-6_6

explores technological trends, governance models, ethical frameworks, and collaborative strategies that will make AI systems to boost individuals and communities. At the same time, it will also enhance creativity, support decision-making, and promote human growth in a responsible and equitable way.

6.2 Technological Innovations Reforming the Future

6.2.1 Evolving Model Architectures and Capabilities

Generative AI models are going to be extremely sophisticated, context-aware, and efficient. Current generation models have started integrating multiple modalities such as text, images, video, audio, and sensor data to generate content more aligned, more coherent, and richer with user expectations. Next generation GAI model will make the outputs more versatile and exactly aligned with user thoughts. Advanced models such as transformer-based models, diffusion models, and GANs will expand the boundaries of high quality and creativity content generation.

Contextual understanding demonstrated by these models will be far better, allowing the models to understand user inputs alongside socio-cultural impacts and dynamic surroundings. This development will enhance the capabilities of generative AI, enabling it to behave as a more understanding and sympathetic companion in creative, scholarly, and professional activities.

6.2.2 Advancement in Explainability and Interpretability

One of the crucial future directions is the development of AI systems and its decision-making ability and it must be ensured that the system is transparent and interpretable. Growth in explainable AI (XAI) will assist users to understand the functionality of AI-based system and its generated content. It will enhance trust and facilitate better human-AI collaboration. It is expected that future tools will provide real-time explanations, attractive visualizations, and interactive controls that will help users to understand how the AI has generated specific outputs, identified biases, and modified results as needed.

6.2.3 Privacy-Focused Technologies

Privacy concerns are most important property in GAI as GAI relies on personal and sensitive data heavily. Federated learning, homomorphic encryption, and differential privacy will be standard components of AI development. Models should learn from decentralized data without compromising individual privacy. These technologies must support ethical data usage, minimize risk of breaches, and strengthen users with greater control over their personal information.

6.2.4 *Real-Time Human-AI Collaboration*

In the future, we expect the development of generative AI systems capable of engaging in real-time dialog with users. Current AI assistants will be able to co-create content, provide contextual recommendations, and even adjust their responses based on a user's communication style and preferences. These systems will use developments in natural language understanding, affective computing, and adaptive learning to enable more productive partnerships between humans and AI.

6.3 Ethical and Societal Aspects

6.3.1 *Persistent Bias and Fairness Issues*

Regardless of how much technology progresses, the possibility of bias existing in the model's training data, architecture, or implementation will remain a key concern. The focus of future work will be on designing comprehensive frameworks for discovering and eliminating biases throughout the entire AI process, from data gathering to result presentation. Such systems require external evaluation for equity and inclusivity, enabling feedback from impacted communities and stakeholders to be actively integrated.

Moreover, future advancements in generative AI must include consideration of overlapping of social categories that affect a person's ability or identity, such as gender, race, or disability, in order to prevent existing societal inequities.

6.3.2 *Improving Accountability and Legal Frameworks*

The expansion of generative AI systems complicates various issues related to accountability. Laws will be formulated and applied regarding the liability for harm caused, documenting, providing clarity for transparency policies, and having proper accountability mechanisms for the AI's misused functions. Responsibility will need to be undertaken by those using the AI in civil society regarding the ethical governance of AI, capturing the AI's decision-making processes, and having policies on responsible advancement. International collaboration will be important in uniformity in the laws since AI systems are influenced by multicultural inputs.

6.3.3 *Dealing with Misinformation and Malicious Use*

The ability to produce realistic synthetic media of real AI increases the proactive risks of misinformation, manipulation and public trust deficit. Future counters will include AI-powered detection tools, digital watermarks for AI-related materials and public education campaign promoting media literacy. Users and platforms will collaborate to implement the authenticity standards while protecting the freedom of expression and privacy.

6.4 Human Empowerment Through Generative AI

Generative AI is helping people of diverse backgrounds specially the marginalized section of society by providing them required information, knowledge which help them in making fast decisions resulting in their Empowerment and growth.

Below are some merits of Generative AI.

6.4.1 *Equitable Access to Creativity and Knowledge Production*

Human-centric generative AI provides equitable access to creative tools and knowledge production. By lowering technical barriers and enabling intuitive interfaces, AI can empower individuals from diverse backgrounds to express themselves artistically, innovate scientifically, and contribute to cultural discourse.

In education, generative AI will support personalized learning experiences tailored to individual strengths, interests, and challenges. It will provide tutors, mentors, and collaborators that adapt to learners' evolving needs, fostering lifelong learning and skill development.

6.4.2 *Supporting Accessibility and Inclusion*

Future generative AI will play a vital role in enhancing accessibility for people with disabilities and marginalized groups. AI-powered communication aids, language translation, and content adaptation tools will bridge gaps in communication and participation. By integrating cultural sensitivity and localization features, AI systems can better serve global communities and respect diverse identities.

6.4.3 *Boosting User Agency and Control*

A cornerstone of human-centric AI is ensuring that users maintain meaningful control over AI interactions and outputs. Future systems will incorporate customizable settings that allow users to define AI behavior boundaries, ethical preferences, and output constraints. This empowerment fosters trust and supports users' autonomy, enabling them to collaborate with AI as partners rather than passive consumers.

6.5 Governance, Regulation, and Multistakeholder Collaboration

To ensure safe and beneficial environment, AI require rules, regulation and collaboration from all stakeholders which includes government bodies, industries, policymakers, academicians, and functional experts. To accomplish this, following practices should be adopted.

6.5.1 *Multi-level Governance Models*

Keeping generative AI in check has to happen on several levels at once, with governments, tech firms, researchers, and everyday people all playing a part. Future rules should still push innovation forward while shielding human rights, privacy, and fairness from new harms. To stay in sync, lawmakers can team up with ethical boards, run public pilot projects, and open real channels for citizens to speak in policy talks.

6.5.2 *Standardization and Certification*

Harmonizing worldwide standards and a clear badge-of-honor process will help make human-centered generative AI accountable and plug-and-play. These benchmarks will address data fairness, transparency, privacy, and security, giving firms a compass and earning public's trust over time. Outside auditors and independent certifiers will be key in testing compliance, spotting room to grow, and rewarding shiny projects that keep moving the goalposts.

6.5.3 Community Engagement and Public Awareness

Ongoing outreach to a wide range of groups-students, workers, AI users, ethicists, policy makers, and people historically left out of tech conversations-remains critical if tomorrow's AI is to reflect shared public values. Well-designed awareness campaigns and classroom materials give individuals the tools they need to examine, question, and use AI systems safely and fairly. When all voices are heard, governance becomes more democratic and the risk of new forms of technological exclusion shrinks.

6.6 Challenges and Opportunities in Future

Collaborative involvement of all stakeholders including marginalized group enhances democratization of AI Technology and prevents technical gap among them. Although advancement in AI providing benefits to certain section of society but probability of misuse of AI in politics, military and medical science has been increased. The details encapsulated below.

6.6.1 Balancing Innovation with Ethical Responsibility

The pressure to push AI capabilities forward will always bump up against the need to limit harm, and that tension is unlikely to fade anytime soon. Meeting it calls for forward-looking ethics reviews, open reports on research choices, and regular conversations that include developers, regulators, and the communities most affected. Organizations therefore need to adopt innovation policies that place people's safety and dignity ahead of short-term profit or prestige.

6.6.2 Managing AI's Environmental Impact

Larger generative models demand runaway electricity and cooling, turning data centers into major carbon sources if care is not taken. Future work must therefore explore lightweight architectures, smarter batch schedules, and hardware that sleeps when idle, along with cloud partners that promise renewable power. Finding that balance between society's hopes for smarter tools and the planet's limits will be one of the hallmark challenges of the next decade.

6.6.3 Adapting to Societal and Cultural Shifts

Generative AI should grow side by side with evolving social norms and diverse cultural backgrounds. Continuous checks, user feedback, and flexible updates must work together so that these tools stay relevant, respectful, and in tune with varied human values around the globe.

6.7 Vision for a Human-Centric AI Future

The long-term dream for human-centered generative AI is simple: technology should lift what people can do, while protecting dignity, diversity, and democratic ideals. In that world, AI systems aim to be

- **transparent and explainable**, so people can trust and fix problems together,
- **fair and inclusive**, actively reducing bias and giving power to overlooked voices,
- **private, safe, and secure**, guarding users control and keeping data clean,
- **guided by strong laws and clear ethics**, making designers and owners accountable,
- **adaptive, context-aware, and multilingual**, tuning itself to local customs and tone, and
- **affordable and easy to use**, opening A.I.s value to everyone, including the poor.

If developers, policymakers, and communities lift these principles into practice, generative AI can help build a more creative, equitable, and thriving society for all people.

6.8 Conclusion

The road ahead for human-centered generative AI looks exciting, yet it is also tangled. Realizing that vision calls for all of us—engineers, ethicists, lawmakers, and communities—to agree on core values, share knowledge across fields, and keep asking how the technology shapes our lives. As generative AI slips into everyday apps, its code and culture must still honor rights, celebrate diversity, and promote the public good.

In this chapter we have sketched the tech breakthroughs, moral questions, policy ideas, and cross-sector partnerships that could steer human-centered generative AI forward. Moving forward, we need to guide the technology with active, informed care so that its power translates into real gains in personal agency, artistic spark, and lasting social progress.

MIX
Papier aus verantwortungsvollen Quellen
Paper from responsible sources
FSC® C105338

If you have any concerns about our products,
you can contact us on
ProductSafety@springernature.com

In case Publisher is established outside the EU,
the EU authorized representative is:
Springer Nature Customer Service Center GmbH
Europaplatz 3, 69115 Heidelberg, Germany

Printed by Libri Plureos GmbH
in Hamburg, Germany